THE FOOLPROOF
BREAD MACHINE COOKBOOK
FOR BEGINNERS

Daisy Collins

ISBN 979-8-39-363170-3

TABLE OF CONTENT

Introduction 5

Chapter 1: Getting To Know Your Bread Machine 6

Chapter 2: The Bread-Making Process 9

Tips And Tricks 10

Troubleshooting Common Issues 11

Faqs 12

Conversion Tables 13

Chapter 3: Basic Bread Recipes 14

1. Country White Bread 14
2. Milk & Honey Bread 14
3. Simple Bread Recipe 14
4. Cinnamon Bread 15
5. Milky White Buttery Bread 16
6. Molasses Rye Bread 16
7. Sweet Basic Bread 17
8. Cornmeal Bread 17
9. Peanut Butter Bread 18
10. Onion Bread 18
11. Everyday Half Wheat Bread 19
12. Spelt Everyday Bread 19
13. Oatmeal Everyday Bread 19

Chapter 4: Whole Wheat Bread Recipes 21

14. Cocoa Whole Wheat Bread 21
15. Cajun Classic Bread 21
16. Quinoa & Whole Wheat Bread 22
17. Whole Wheat Bread With Flaxseed 22
18. Herbed Whole Wheat Bread Recipe 23
19. Sweet Potato Bread 23
20. Black & Green Olive Whole Wheat Bread 24
21. Sesame Whole Wheat Bread 24
22. Whole Wheat Cinnamon Raisin Bread 25
23. Whole Wheat Bread With Sunflower Seed 26
24. Simple Whole Wheat Bread 26
25. Whole Grain Seed Loaf 26
26. Whole Wheat Banana Bread 27

Chapter 5: Breakfast Bread Recipes 28

27. French Bread With A Crust 28
28. Bran Bread With Oat 28
29. Tomato & Olive Bread 29
30. Amish White Bread Loaf 29
31. Lightweight Oat Bread 30
32. Whole Grain Wheat Bread 30
33. Soft Everyday Bread 31
34. Caraway Rye Bread Loaf 31

35. Simple Breakfast Milk Bread 32
36. Potato Crust Bread Loaf 32
37. Breakfast Cranberry & Orange Bread 33
38. Flaxseed Whole Wheat Bread 33
39. Sunflower Seed Bran Bread 34

Chapter 6: Spice, Herb & Vegetable Bread Recipes 35

40. Garlic Herb Bread 35
41. Italian Herb & Cheese Bread 35
42. Potato Whole Wheat Bread 36
43. Kalamata Olive Oil Bread 36
44. Star Anise Seed Bread 37
45. Orange Spice Bread 37
46. Toasted Walnut Bread 38
47. Chives & Sour Cream Bread 39
48. Caramelized Onion & Yeast Bread 39
49. Sunflower Seed Yeast Bread 40
50. Cajun Herb Bread 40
51. Roasted Garlic Clove Bread 41
52. Rosemary Italian Peasant Bread 42

Chapter 7: Cheese Bread Recipes 43

53. Cream Cheese Yeast Bread 43
54. Sharp Cheese Yeast Bread 43
55. Feta Cheese Yeast Bread 44
56. Jalapeno & Cheese Bread 44
57. Ricotta Cheese & Yeast Bread 45
58. Pepperoni & Cheese Bread 45
59. Cottage Cheese & Dill Bread 46
60. Simple Oregano & Cheese Bread 46
61. Cheese & Scallion Bread 47
62. Easy Cottage Cheese Bread 47
63. Cheese Bread With Pepperoni 48
64. Cheese Bread with Jalapeno 48
65. Bacon & Cheddar Cheese Bread 49

Chapter 8: Quick Bread Recipes 50

66. Pumpkin Spice Quick Bread 50
67. Cranberry Quick Bread Loaf 50
68. Zucchini Quick Bread Loaf 51
69. Quick Banana Bread Loaf 51
70. Classic White Bread With No Yeast 52
71. Cornmeal Quick Bread 52
72. No Yeast Quick Flatbread 53
73. No Yeast Tutti Frutti Bread Cake 53
74. Pumpkin Pie Spice Quick Bread 54
75. Jalapeno Cheese Quick Cornbread 55

76. Yeast Free Quick Chocolate Cake 55

77. Moist Quick Chocolate Cake 56

78. Quick Zucchini Bread Loaf 56

Chapter 9: Sweet Bread Recipes 58

79. Nutty Banana Bread 58

80. Date Bread With Cinnamon 58

81. Pumpernickel Bread 59

82. Cream Cheese Sweet Bread 59

83. Sweet Fruit Bread 60

84. Cranberry & Oats Bread 61

85. Applesauce & Oat Bread 61

86. Sweet Orange & Cranberry Bread 62

87. Sweet Portuguese Bread 62

88. Sweet Rum Raisin Bread 63

89. Sweet & Spicy Fruit Bread 63

90. Pecan & Raisin Bread 64

91. Cherry & Pecan Bread 65

Chapter 10: Gluten-Free Bread Recipes 66

92. Easy Gluten Free Bread 66

93. Healthy Gluten Free Bread 66

94. Gluten Free Einkorn-Style Bread 67

95. Whole Grain Gluten Free Bread 67

96. Raisin Bran Bread Loaf 68

97. Gluten Free White Bread 68

98. Gluten Free Almond Bread 69

99. Simple Gluten Free Bread 70

100. Oat Rice Gluten Free Bread 70

101. Vegan Bread Machine Loaf 71

102. Linseed Gluten Free Bread 71

103. Cornbread Gluten Free Loaf 72

104. Rice Gluten Free Bread 73

Chapter 11: Pizza & Focaccia Bread Recipes 74

105. Simple Pizza Bread Machine Dough 74

106. Super Easy Pizza Bread 74

107. Sourdough Pizza Dough Bread 75

108. Sparkling Water Pizza Dough 75

109. Italian Pizza Crust 76

110. Rosemary & Garlic Focaccia 77

111. Herb Focaccia Bread 77

112. Sun-Dried Tomato Focaccia Bread 78

113. Onion & Cheese Focaccia 79

114. Caramelized Onion Focaccia Bread 79

115. Olive Focaccia Bread 80

116. Onion & Herbs Focaccia 81

117. Focaccia Flat Bread 81

Chapter 12: Sourdough Bread Recipes 83

118. Easy Sourdough Bread 83

119. Tangy Sourdough Bread 83

120. Bread Machine Sourdough 83

121. Rosemary Sourdough Bread 84

122. Rye Sourdough Bread 84

123. Basic Sourdough Bread 85

124. Sourdough Bread With A Twist 86

125. Multigrain Sourdough Bread 86

126. Overnight Sourdough Bread 87

127. Czech Sourdough Bread 87

128 Amish Sourdough Bread 88

129. Sourdough Bread With Beer 88

130. Sourdough Bread With Oatmeal 89

Chapter 13: Holiday Bread Recipes 90

131. Pure Whole Wheat Bread 90

132. Carrot & Thyme Yeast Bread 90

133. Oatmeal & Honey Multigrain Bread 91

134. Moist Peanut Butter Bread 91

135. Cereal Grain Bread 92

136. Chocolate & Cinnamon Bread 92

137. Golden Syrup Bread 93

138. Zucchini Whole Wheat Bread 93

139. Christmas Limpa Bread 94

140. Special Panettone Bread 94

141. Easy Molasses Loaf Bread 95

142. Cheesy Rosemary Bread 96

143. Persimmon Pulp Bread 96

144. Quick Banana Nut Bread 97

145 Healthy Einkorn Bread Loaf 97

146. Almond High Protein Bread 98

147. Semisweet Chocolate Bread 98

148. White Potato Bread 99

149. Fragrant Garlic Bread 99

150. Hawaiian Pineapple Bread 100

151. Special Multigrain Bread 101

152. Simple Sugar Free Bread 101

Conclusion 103

Bonus Chapter: 104

Cleaning And Maintenance Of A Bread Machine 104

How Do You Store Your Bread Machine? 104

Introduction

"Bread is the most fundamentally satisfying of all foods, and good bread with fresh butter, the greatest of feasts."
-James Beard

We all need bread on our tables, and there is nothing more tempting than the aroma of freshly baked, homemade bread. Before bread machines, the idea of "homemade" bread was just a dream, as traditional methods of bread-making required expertise that not all of us have. Now with a bread machine resting on your countertop, you can measure and add ingredients to it, and the machine will do the rest for you. How amazing is that? From mixing to kneading, leavening, and baking the bread- this nifty kitchen appliance can do it all. With its various bread-making functions, it automates the entire bread-making process while you sit and relax on your couch.

Besides the ease and convenience of baking the bread for you, bread makers are also good at providing consistent results, satisfying textures, and a variety of bread due to their multiple functions. Perhaps, this one machine can open the doors of limitless possibilities for you as you can practically make any loaf of your choice by just adding the right amount of ingredients. And that's where this ultimate guide on Bread machines with amazing bread recipes comes into play.

Whether you are an expert baker or a novice cook, you are still learning to bake perfect bread; this cookbook has a detailed Bread machine guide that will help you steer through the entire process of getting to know this machine and the techniques to use. Moreover, it has all the delicious loaf recipes that you can bake in your bread maker- from basic white bread to whole wheat, sweet, French, and gluten-free bread. And this collection of recipes is diverse enough to keep your bread-baking needs covered for up to 1,500 days. Just imagine the variety you are going to add to your menu. So without further ado! Let's get started!

Chapter 1: Getting to Know Your Bread Machine

Bread machines, also known as bread makers, were first introduced in the 1980s. The idea behind the bread machine was to provide a convenient way for people to make fresh bread at home without having to do all the work by hand. The first bread machines were simple and could only make basic white bread. They had limited settings and required a lot of trial and error to get the perfect loaf. However, as technology improved, bread machines became more sophisticated, with a wider range of settings and features.

In the 1990s, the popularity of bread machines grew as more and more people embraced the convenience of making bread at home. Manufacturers began to offer bread machines with more advanced features, such as automatic yeast dispensers, gluten-free settings, and multiple loaf sizes. Today, bread machines are widely available and come in a range of styles and price points. They continue to be popular with home bakers who appreciate the convenience and versatility of these appliances.

How Does a Bread Machine Work?

A bread machine is an electric appliance designed to make bread-making easier and more convenient. It consists of a bread pan, a kneading paddle, and a heating element that work together to produce the perfect loaf of bread. All you need to do is add the ingredients to the pan in the correct order and let the machine do the rest. In a very short time, you will have a freshly baked loaf of bread that looks and tastes like it came straight out of a bakery! With a bread machine, the possibilities for bread types and flavors are endless. Whether you prefer classic white bread or a hearty, multigrain loaf, you can easily customize your bread to your liking. Plus, with gluten-free options available, even those with dietary restrictions can enjoy freshly baked bread at home. So, why settle for store-bought bread when you can have delicious, homemade bread with a bread machine? It's easy, convenient, and the perfect way to impress your family and pals with your baking skills.

The process begins with the mixing of ingredients in a mixing chamber or bowl. The machine ensures that all the ingredients are combined evenly to form a smooth dough. After mixing, the dough is left to rise in the bread machine. During this process, the yeast in the dough produces carbon dioxide- CO_2, which makes the dough expand and rise. Once the dough has risen, the bread machine kneads it to strengthen the gluten strands and give the bread its structure. After kneading, the bread machine bakes the bread by heating the interior to the appropriate temperature. Finally, the bread machine cools the bread before releasing it from the pan or mixing chamber. Bread machines typically have different settings for different types of bread and crust colors. They also have a timer feature that allows you to set the machine to start at a specific time, so you can have fresh bread ready when you wake up or come home from work. Overall, bread machines make it easy and convenient to make fresh bread at home, even if you have limited time or baking experience.

Why We Love Bread Machines?

Convenience: Forget about mixing and kneading the bread ingredients with your hands. The bread machine can do it for you. Now all you need to do is to understand the functions of this machine, put in the ingredients and select the right program to make the machine work for you.

Consistent results: A bread maker can help ensure that your bread turns out consistently good every time. The machine will mix, knead, rise, and bake the bread according to a preset program, which helps to ensure that the bread is evenly baked and has a consistent texture.

Saves money: Making bread at home using a bread maker can be much cheaper than buying bread from a store or bakery. You can buy ingredients in bulk and make larger batches of bread, which can save you money in the long run.

Bakes healthy homemade bread: Homemade bread made with whole grains can be a healthier option than store-bought bread, which may contain preservatives and other additives. You can also control the amount of salt and sugar in your bread when making it at home.

Bakes Variety of Bread loaves: A bread maker can be used to make a wide range of bread, including white, wheat, rye, and sourdough bread, as well as specialty bread like gluten-free or vegan bread. This allows you to experiment with different recipes and flavors to find your favorites.

Bread Machine Cycles

Bread machines have cycles to automate the bread-making process. Each cycle represents a specific step in the process, such as mixing, kneading, rising, and baking. The cycles ensure that the ingredients are properly. A bread machine typically has several cycles that allow you to make different types of bread and dough. Here are some common cycles you might find on a bread machine:

Kneading cycle: This cycle is designed to mix and knead the ingredients to form a smooth dough. It usually takes around 20 to 30 minutes.

Rising cycle: During this cycle, the dough is left to rise. The bread machine creates a warm, humid environment that helps the dough to rise properly. This cycle usually takes around 1 to 2 hours.

Punch-down cycle: After the dough has risen, the bread machine will punch it down to release any air pockets that may have formed. This helps to ensure an even texture throughout the bread.

Baking cycle: During this cycle, the bread machine heats up and bakes the bread. The length of this cycle can vary depending on the type of bread being made, but it typically takes around 1 to 2 hours.

Keep warm cycle: Once the bread has finished baking, some bread machines have a keep warm cycle that will keep the bread warm for a period of time. This is useful if you want to serve the bread right away.

In addition to these cycles, some bread machines may have additional settings that allow you to make different types of bread, such as whole wheat, gluten-free, or artisan bread. Some machines also have a delay start function, which allows you to set the machine to start making bread at a later time, so you can have fresh bread ready when you want it.

Selecting The Right Bread Program and Settings

Choosing the right bread program and settings on your bread machine can be the key to making the perfect loaf of bread. Here is how you can select the right program and settings for your bread machine:

Follow the exact recipe: Before selecting a program, make sure you have the right recipe for the type of bread you want to make. Different types of bread require different ingredients and settings, so be sure to follow the recipe carefully.

Choose the right program: Most bread machines come with pre-programmed settings for different types of bread, like white, whole wheat, or gluten-free. Choose the program that corresponds to the type of bread you are making.

Select the crust color: Most bread machines allow you to select the desired crust color, such as light, medium, or dark. Choose the crust color that you prefer.

Adjust the loaf size: Some bread machines allow you to choose the size of the loaf you want to make, typically ranging from one to three pounds. Choose the size that's appropriate for your needs.

Customize the settings: Some bread machines allow you to customize the settings, such as the kneading time, rising time, or baking time. If you have a recipe that requires specific settings, be sure to adjust them accordingly.

Use the delay timer: If your bread machine has a delay timer, you can set it to start baking at a specific time, such as early in the morning or when you get home from work. This is a convenient feature if you want fresh bread ready at a specific time.

Things To Consider Before Buying a Bread Machine

If you haven't made up your mind about which model of bread machine you are going to bring home. Then hold your horses! A bread machine is a great one-time investment that is going to meet all your bread-baking needs. So before landing on any final decision, consider the following few important factors and then make up your mind about it:

The Size Matters

Bread machines come in different sizes, so think about how much bread you want to make at a time. If you have a large family or like to bake in bulk, a larger machine may be a better fit.

The Bread Functions

Some bread machines come with pre-programmed settings for different types of bread, such as white, whole wheat, or gluten-free. Others allow you to program your own settings, giving you more control over the baking process.

Count the Kneading Paddles

Some bread machines come with a single kneading paddle, while others have dual paddles. Dual paddles can be more effective at kneading the dough, but they can also make it harder to remove the bread from the pan.

Crust Color Settings

Most bread machines allow you to choose the desired crust color, such as light, medium, or dark. Make sure the machine you choose has the crust color options you prefer.

Additional Features

Most bread machines come with additional features such as a delay timer, a keep-warm function, or a fruit and nut dispenser. Consider which features are important to you and choose a machine that has them.

Reviews Are a Must Read

Finally, be sure to read reviews from other customers to get an idea of how well the bread machine performs and whether it's worth the investment.

Chapter 2: The Bread-Making Process

With a bread maker, you simply add your ingredients, select your settings, and let the machine do the work for you. This makes it a perfect option for busy people who love the taste of fresh bread but don't have the time or energy to go through the entire bread making process by hand. The bread maker allows you to enjoy the delicious aroma of baking bread in your home, without any of the hassle or mess. In this article, we'll take a closer look at the benefits of using a bread maker, as well as some tips for getting the best results from your machine. Since different bread machines have their own settings suggested by the manufacturer, so here without getting into the details on how to use your bread machine I am about to share some of the most useful measurement tips, tricks, altitude adjustment techniques, troubleshooting and faqs about the whole process of using a bread machine like a pro!

Measuring Ingredients Correctly

A slight change in measurement can ruin the entire bread recipe. It is, therefore, crucial to measure each and every ingredient accurately.

- **Use the appropriate measuring cups and spoons.** It's important to use standard measuring cups and spoons rather than estimating or using random kitchen utensils. Measuring cups and spoons can be purchased at most grocery stores or online.
- **Use a scale.** Measuring the bread ingredients by weight is more accurate than measuring by volume, especially for flour. A kitchen scale is a great investment and will ensure consistent results every time.
- **Fluff the flour.** When measuring flour, it's important to fluff it up first with a spoon or whisk. This will loosen up the flour and prevent it from packing down in the measuring cup, which can result in too much flour and a dry or dense loaf of bread.
- **Level off the ingredients.** After measuring the ingredient, level it off with a flat edge, such as a butter knife, to ensure you have the exact amount needed for the recipe.
- **Add ingredients in the order specified.** Most bread machine recipes will specify the order in which ingredients should be added. Typically, liquid ingredients are added first, followed by dry ingredients, with the yeast being added last.

How To Store the Baked Bread?

If you have made a delicious loaf of bread in your bread machine but can't eat it all at once, freezing is a great way to store it for later. Before freezing your bread, make sure it has cooled completely. This will stop the moisture from building up in the bag and keep the bread fresh. If you are planning to use your bread for sandwiches or toast, slice it before freezing. That will make it easier for you to thaw and use later. To wrap the bread, wrap it tightly in plastic wrap or aluminum foil or use a freezer-safe bag. Ensure that there is no air inside the bag, as this can cause a freezer burn. Write the date on the bag or wrap, so you know when you froze the bread. This will let you keep track of how long it has been in the freezer. Place the plastic-wrapped bread in the freezer and keep it there for up to three months. To thaw frozen bread, simply take it out of the freezer and let it achieve room temperature on the counter. You can also toast it straight from the freezer or microwave it for a few seconds to warm it up. With these tips, you can enjoy your homemade bread for weeks to come!

Tips and Tricks

The first few trials are destined for failure when it comes to exploring the features of your new bread machine. Often your bread turns out to be too soft, too hard, dry, or undercooked. There are several ways in which this whole process can go south ways, but the following tips and tricks have your back- they will help you achieve great results by avoiding the common mistakes while using a bread machine:

- **Add ingredients in the correct order**: Most bread machine recipes specify the order in which ingredients should be added. Typically, liquid ingredients are added first, followed by dry ingredients, with the yeast being added last. The correct order of the ingredients is important for getting the right texture of the dough or bread; that's why most bread machine manufacturers emphasize this point.

- **Use the right flour**: Different bread machine recipes call for different types of flour, and it is important to consider the suggested type of flour for each recipe as it makes a huge difference in the final outcome. If the recipe calls for all-purpose flour- use it; if it calls for bread flour, then go for it.

- **Measure ingredients accurately:** Accurate measurement of ingredients is important when making bread in a bread machine. Use a suitable kitchen scale or measuring cups and spoons to ensure precise measurements.

- **Don't overfill the bread machine**: Follow the manufacturer's instructions regarding the maximum amount of flour and liquid that can be used in the bread machine. Overfilling the machine can cause the dough to rise too much and overflow, resulting in a mess.

- **Use the yeast properly:** If a recipe calls for the use of yeast, add it as per the manufacturer's instructions. If you are using active dry yeast, it needs to be activated in lukewarm warm water before being added to the other ingredients. And if you are using instant yeast, then you can add it to the flour and other ingredients directly without activating.

- **Keep an eye on the dough:** It's important to monitor the dough during the mixing and rising phases to ensure that it's not too dry or too wet. If your bread dough is too dry, add a little more liquid. If your dough is too wet, sprinkle some more flour.

- **Choose the right cycle:** Bread machines come with a variety of cycles, including basic, whole wheat, dough, and rapid. Choose the cycle that best suits the type of bread you are making.

- **Use the right crust setting**: Bread machines also have different crust settings, ranging from light to dark. Choose the setting that gives you the crust you prefer.

- **Let the bread cool before slicing:** Letting the bread cool for at least 15 minutes before slicing will make it easier to cut and will help prevent it from becoming soggy.

Troubleshooting Common Issues

Bread makers are a great appliance to have in your kitchen for making fresh, homemade bread. However, like any appliance, they can experience issues from time to time. Here are some common issues that you may have to deal with while using a bread machine:

The bread is not rising:

- Check the expiration date of your yeast and make sure it's fresh.
- Make sure the yeast is being added to the dough in the correct order and that it's not coming into contact with the salt.
- Check that the water temperature is correct. Too hot or too cold water can kill the yeast.
- Ensure the dough has the correct consistency. If it's too dry or too wet, it may not rise properly.

The bread rises too much, then deflates:

There are several possible reasons why your bread may deflate after rising, but the two most common causes are under-kneading and over-proofing. Under-kneading can result in a weak gluten network that is unable to support the weight of the rising dough while over-proofing can lead to excessive gas production and eventual collapse of the dough structure.

- To solve this issue, one possible solution is to punch down the dough to release excess gas and redistribute the yeast and other ingredients.
- This will help to reset the dough structure and give it a chance to rise again properly.
- Another approach is to carefully monitor the kneading and proofing process to ensure that the dough has been sufficiently developed and allowed to rise at the appropriate pace.
- This may involve adjusting the amount of yeast or other ingredients, as well as tweaking the kneading and proofing times and temperatures as needed.

The bread is too dense:

- Check the expiration date of your yeast and make sure it's fresh.
- Make sure you are using the correct flour for the recipe.
- Make sure you are using the correct amount of yeast and flour. Too much flour or too little yeast can lead to dense bread.
- Make sure you are not adding too much salt, as it can inhibit the yeast.

The bread maker is making strange noises:

- Check that the bread pan is properly seated in the bread maker.
- Make sure the kneading blade is properly attached and not hitting the sides of the pan.
- Check that the bread maker is level and not rocking.

The bread is burning:

- Check that you are not using too much sugar, as it can cause the bread to burn.
- Make sure you are using the correct setting for the recipe.
- Check that the crust color setting is not too dark.

The bread is too dry:

- Make sure you are measuring the ingredients accurately.
- Check that you are not using too much flour or too little liquid.
- Ensure the dough has the correct consistency.

These are some common issues and troubleshooting tips for bread makers. If you are still experiencing issues, consult the instruction manual or contact the manufacturer for assistance.

Faqs

Q: Is it difficult to use a bread machine?
A: Not at all! Bread machines are designed to be easy to use, even for beginners. Simply add the ingredients, select the appropriate settings, and let the machine do the work.

Q: Do I need to use bread flour in my bread machine?
A: While bread flour is ideal for making bread, you can use all-purpose flour in your bread machine if you don't have bread flour on hand. Just keep in mind that the texture and rise of your bread may be slightly different.

Q: Can I make gluten-free bread in a bread machine?
A: Yes! Many bread machines come with a gluten-free setting, or you can use a gluten-free recipe and select the appropriate settings for your machine.

Q: Can I make the dough in my bread machine and then bake that dough in the oven?
A: Absolutely! Many bread machines have a dough cycle that allows you to mix and knead the dough, but then you can shape it by hand and bake it in the oven.

Q: Can I add mix-ins like nuts or dried fruit to my bread machine dough?
A: Yes, you can! Just be sure to add them at the appropriate time in the cycle, usually towards the end of the kneading process.

Q: How do I clean my bread machine?
A: Most bread machines come with a non-stick bread pan that can be easily cleaned with warm soapy water. Be sure to wipe down the exterior of the machine as well.

Q: How long will bread stay fresh in a bread machine?
A: Freshly baked bread is best consumed within 1-2 days. To extend the life of your bread, store it in an airtight container or freeze it for later use.

Q: Can I make other things besides bread in my bread machine?
A: Some bread machines come with additional settings for making things like pizza dough, jam, and even cake! Be sure to consult your machine's user manual for specific instructions.

Altitude Adjustment

Altitude can have a significant impact on the whole process of bread making, especially for those living at higher elevations. At higher altitudes, the air pressure is comparatively lower, and this can cause bread dough to rise too quickly or not rise enough. As a result, bread made at high altitudes can turn out too dense or too dry. To adjust for altitude when using a bread machine, you may need to make some modifications to the recipe or the baking process. Here is how you can make adjustments to get the best results:

Use less yeast: At higher altitudes, the lower air pressure can cause bread dough to rise faster. To slow down the rising process, you may need to use less yeast than the recipe calls for.

Reduce sugar and fat: Sugar and fat can also speed up the rising process, so you may need to reduce the amount of sugar and fat in your recipe.

Increase liquid: At high altitudes, the air is drier, and this can cause bread to dry out more quickly. To counteract this, you may need to increase the amount of liquid in your recipe.

Increase baking time and temperature: The lower air pressure at high altitudes can cause bread to take longer to bake. You need to increase the baking time and temperature to ensure that the bread is fully cooked.

Experiment: Altitude adjustments can be tricky, and the best approach may vary depending on your specific location and the recipe you are using. Don't be afraid to experiment with different adjustments until you find which adjustment changes work best for you.

Conversion Tables

Flour

1 cup	125 grams
3/4 cup	94 grams
2/3 cup	83 grams
1/2 cup	63 grams
1/3 cup	42 grams
1/4 cup	31 grams
1 tablespoon	8 grams
1 teaspoon	3 grams

Granulated Sugar

1 cup	200 grams
3/4 cup	150 grams
2/3 cup	133 grams
1/2 cup	100 grams
1/3 cup	67 grams
1/4 cup	50 grams
1 tablespoon	12.5 grams
1 teaspoon	4 grams

Powdered Sugar

1 cup	120 grams
3/4 cup	90 grams
2/3 cup	80 grams
1/2 cup	60 grams
1/3 cup	40 grams
1/4 cup	30 grams
1 tablespoon	8 grams
1 teaspoon	3 grams

Cocoa powder

1 cup	85 grams
3/4 cup	64 grams
2/3 cup	56.6 grams
1/2 cup	42.5 grams
1/3 cup	28.3 grams
1/4 cup	21.25 grams
1 tablespoon	5.3 grams
1 teaspoon	1.8 grams

Butter

1 cup	2 sticks	8 ounces	226 grams
3/4 cup	1 1/2 sticks	6 ounces	170 grams
2/3 cup	1 1/3 sticks	5.33 ounces	151 grams
1/2 cup	1 stick	4 ounces	113 grams
1/3 cup	0.67 sticks	2.67 ounces	75 grams
1/4 cup	0.5 sticks	2 ounces	56.7 grams
1 tablespoon		0.5 ounces	14.2 grams
1 teaspoon		0.17 ounces	4.7 grams

Milk

1 cup	8 fluid ounces	240 ml
3/4 cup	6 fluid ounces	180 ml
2/3 cup	5.3 fluid ounces	160 ml
1/2 cup	4 fluid ounces	120 ml
1/3 cup	2.7 fluid ounces	80 ml
1/4 cup	2 fluid ounces	60 ml
1 tablespoon	0.5 fluid ounces	15 ml
1 teaspoon	0.17 fluid ounces	5 ml

Heavy Cream

1 cup	8 fluid ounces	240 ml	226 grams
3/4 cup	6 fluid ounces	180 ml	170 grams
2/3 cup	5.3 fluid ounces	160 ml	151 grams
1/2 cup	4 fluid ounces	120 ml	113 grams
1/3 cup	2.7 fluid ounces	80 ml	75 grams
1/4 cup	2 fluid ounces	60 ml	56.5 grams
1 tablespoon	0.5 fluid ounces	15 ml	14.2 grams
1 teaspoon	0.17 fluid ounces	5 ml	4.7 grams

Chapter 3: Basic Bread Recipes

1. Country White Bread

Prep Time: 20 minutes or less
Ready Time: 2 hours 20 minutes

12 Slices/1 ½ pounds
- 1 teaspoon salt
- 1 cup bread flour
- 4 teaspoons olive oil
- 1 ½ teaspoons sugar
- ¼ teaspoon baking soda
- 1 ½ cups lukewarm water
- 2 ½ teaspoons bread machine yeast
- 2 ½ cups all-purpose flour, more as needed

16 Slices/2 pounds
- 1 ½ teaspoon salt
- 1 ½ bread flour
- 5 teaspoons olive oil
- 2 teaspoons sugar
- ½ teaspoon baking soda
- 2 cups lukewarm water
- 3 teaspoons bread machine yeast
- 3 cups all-purpose flour, more as needed

Directions:
1. Place ingredients in the bread machine pan according to the manufacturer's recommended order.
2. Select the Fast setting (if available) and Medium crust on your machine, and Start.
3. When the bread is done, take out the bread after 2 ½ hours and let it cool on a cooling rack.
4. Slice to serve and enjoy!

Nutrition:
Per Serving Calories: 448, Total Fat: 5.6g, Saturated Fat: 0.8g, Carbohydrates: 84.3g, Fiber: 2.6g, Sodium: 664mg, Protein: 13.1g

Tip: Keep a check on your dough during the kneading cycle. Add more flour if the dough is too sticky and add more water if too stiff. Your dough should be soft to get a perfect result.

2. Milk & Honey Bread

Prep Time: 10 minutes or less
Ready Time: 3 hours 25 minutes

12 Slices/1 ½ pounds
- 1 teaspoon salt
- 3 cups bread flour
- 4 tablespoons honey
- 1 cup plus 1 tablespoon milk
- 2 teaspoons active dry yeast
- 3 tablespoons butter, melted

16 Slices/2 pounds
- 1 ½ teaspoon salt
- 4 cups bread flour
- 4 ½ tablespoons honey
- 1 ½ cup plus 1 tablespoon milk
- 2 ½ teaspoons active dry yeast
- 4 tablespoons butter, melted

Directions:
1. Place ingredients in the bread machine pan according to the manufacturer's recommended order.
2. Select the White Bread with the Medium crust setting, and press Start.
3. When the bread is done, take it out from the machine and let it cool on a cooling rack.
4. Slice after 10 minutes and enjoy!

Nutrition:
Per Serving Calories: 502, Total Fat: 10.9g, Saturated Fat: 6.4g, Carbohydrates: 88.3g, Fiber: 3g, Sodium: 966mg, Protein: 12.6g

Tip: If you don't have active dry yeast, you can use bread machine yeast, instant or rapid-rise yeast. But make sure to add the correct quantity: 2 teaspoons of active dry yeast equals 1 ½ teaspoon of other types of yeast. Plus, make certain your yeast is fresh, not old as the bread won't rise.

3. Simple Bread Recipe

Prep Time: 10 minutes or less
Ready Time: 3 hours 25 minutes

12 Slices/1 ½ pounds

- 1 teaspoon salt
- 3 cups white flour
- ¼ cup vegetable oil
- 4 teaspoons white sugar
- 1 cup warm water, 110 degrees F
- 2 ¼ teaspoons bread machine yeast

16 Slices/2 pounds

- 1 ½ teaspoon salt
- 4 cups white flour
- ½ cup vegetable oil
- 4 ½ teaspoons white sugar
- 1 ½ cups warm water, 110 degrees F
- 2 ½ teaspoons bread machine yeast

Directions:

1. Place ingredients in the bread machine pan according to the manufacturer's recommended order.
2. Or simply pour water, sugar, and yeast into a bowl and let it dissolve for 6 minutes.
3. Then add white flour, oil, and salt to the bowl and transfer this mixture to a bread machine pan.
4. Top it with yeast mixture.
5. Select the Basic Bread setting on the machine, and press Start.
6. Once the cycle is complete, let the bread loaf cool for 5 minutes.
7. Slice after 10 minutes and enjoy!

Nutrition:

Per Serving Calories: 482, Total Fat: 14.6g, Saturated Fat: 2.8g, Carbohydrates: 76.2g, Fiber: 2.9g, Sodium: 586mg, Protein: 10.4g

Tip: We don't recommend using canola oil as vegetable oil as it doesn't work well. Or you can substitute vegetable oil with melted butter.

4. Cinnamon Bread

Prep Time: 5 minutes or less
Ready Time: 3 hours 5 minutes

12 Slices/1 ½ pounds

- 2 eggs
- ½ cup raisins
- 1 cup warm water
- 3 cups bread flour
- 1 ½ teaspoons salt
- 3 tablespoons sugar
- 2 tablespoons butter, softened
- 2 teaspoons ground cinnamon
- 1 ½ teaspoons active dry yeast

16 Slices/2 pounds

- 3 eggs
- 1 cup raisins
- 1 ½ cup warm water
- 4 cups bread flour
- 2 teaspoons salt
- 4 tablespoons sugar
- 3 tablespoons butter, softened
- 2 ½ teaspoons ground cinnamon
- 2 teaspoons active dry yeast

Directions:

1. Place ingredients in the bread machine pan according to the manufacturer's recommended order.
2. Or simply pour water into a bread machine pan and add egg and soften butter.
3. Add on top the sugar, salt, and cinnamon.
4. Make a hole in the center and add flour and yeast.
5. Add raisins 10 minutes before the kneading cycle ends.
6. Follow the bread machine manual instructions by selecting the Basic White setting.
7. When the bread is done, take it out and let it cool on a cooling rack.
8. Slice after 10 minutes and enjoy!

Nutrition:

Per Serving Calories: 503, Total Fat: 7.9g, Saturated Fat: 4.2g, Carbohydrates: 96.5g, Fiber: 4.1g, Sodium: 935mg, Protein: 12.3g

Tip: We don't recommend using canola oil as vegetable oil as it doesn't work well. Or you can substitute vegetable oil with melted butter.

5. Milky White Buttery Bread

Prep Time: 5 minutes or less
Ready Time: 2 hours 20 minutes

12 Slices/1 ½ pounds
- A pinch of salt
- 6 teaspoons butter
- 1 cup lukewarm water
- ⅓ cup lukewarm milk
- 1 ½ teaspoons instant yeast
- 6 teaspoons granulated sugar
- 3 ¾ cups Unbleached All-Purpose Flour

16 Slices/2 pounds
- A pinch of salt
- 6 teaspoons butter
- 1 cup lukewarm water
- ⅓ cup lukewarm milk
- 1 ½ teaspoons instant yeast
- 6 teaspoons granulated sugar
- 4 cups Unbleached All-Purpose Flour

Directions:
1. Place ingredients in the bread machine pan according to the manufacturer's recommended order.
2. Select the White Bread setting, and Start.
3. When the bread is done, take it out from the machine and let it cool on a cooling rack.
4. Slice after 10 minutes and enjoy!

Nutrition:
Per Serving Calories: 514, Total Fat: 7.4g, Saturated Fat: 4.1g, Carbohydrates: 97g, Fiber: 3.5g, Sodium: 92mg, Protein: 13.4g

Tip: You can wrap the bread properly and freeze the bread for 3 months. Or wrap it well for it to stay fresh for 4 days on the counter.

6. Molasses Rye Bread

Prep Time: 5 minutes or less
Ready Time: 3 hours 30 minutes

12 Slices/1 ½ pounds
- A pinch of salt
- 1 cup rye flour
- ¼ cup molasses
- 1 cup warm water
- 2 cups bread flour
- 4 teaspoons vegetable oil
- 2 teaspoons active dry yeast

16 Slices/2 pounds
- A pinch of salt
- 1 ½ cup rye flour
- ½ cup molasses
- 1 ½ cups warm water
- 2 ½ cups bread flour
- 4 ½ teaspoons vegetable oil
- 2 ½ teaspoons active dry yeast

Directions:
1. Place ingredients in the bread machine pan according to the manufacturer's recommended order.
2. Or simply pour warm water, molasses, vegetable oil, and salt into your bread machine pan.
3. Next, put the rye flour and bread flour.
4. Make a small hole in the center of the flour and put it in the yeast.
5. Read the instructions in your bread machine manual and select the Rye Bread setting.
6. When the bread is done, take it out and let it cool on a cooling rack.
7. Slice after 10 minutes and enjoy!

Nutrition:
Per Serving Calories: 437, Total Fat: 6.1g, Saturated Fat: 1.1g, Carbohydrates: 85.8g, Fiber: 9.3g, Sodium: 51mg, Protein: 11.7g

Tip: The vegetable oil can be substituted with margarine, butter, olive oil, or even lard. You can store the bread for 3 to 4 days by wrapping it in a sealed plastic bag.

7. Sweet Basic Bread

Prep Time: 10 minutes or less
Ready Time: 3 hours 15 minutes

12 Slices/ 1 ½ pounds
- 1 ½ teaspoons salt
- 3 cups bread flour
- 2 tablespoons honey
- 1 ¼ cups warm water
- 2 tablespoons vegetable oil
- 2 teaspoons active dry yeast

16 Slices/ 2 pounds
- 2 teaspoons salt
- 4 cups bread flour
- 3 tablespoons honey
- 1 ½ cups warm water
- 3 tablespoons vegetable oil
- 2 ½ teaspoons active dry yeast

Directions:
1. Place ingredients in the bread machine pan according to the manufacturer's recommended order.
2. Or simply pour warm water, honey, vegetable oil, and salt into the bread machine pan
3. Add these ingredients on top of the bread flour.
4. Make a small hole in the center of the flour and put the yeast.
5. Select the Basic White Bread setting, and start.
6. When the bread is done, take it out and let it cool on a cooling rack.
7. Slice after 10 minutes and enjoy!

Nutrition:
Per Serving Calories: 439, Total Fat: 7.8g, Saturated Fat: 1.5g, Carbohydrates: 81g, Fiber: 3g, Sodium: 878mg, Protein: 10.5g

Tip: If you want to store the bread for a long time, store it in the freezer. Put it in a storage bag and write down the contents, date and use by date (3 months) as a reminder on the bag. Thaw it an hour before use at room temperature!

8. Cornmeal Bread

Prep Time: 10 minutes or less
Ready Time: 2 hours 10 minutes

12 Slices/1 ½ pounds
- A pinch of salt
- ¾ cup cornmeal
- 2 eggs, organic
- 2 ¾ cups bread flour
- ¾ cup whole wheat flour
- 2 tablespoons light brown
- 2 ½ teaspoons active dry yeast
- 1 ⅓ cups water, room temperature
- 4 teaspoons unsalted butter, softened

16 Slices/2 pounds
- A pinch of salt
- 1 cup cornmeal
- 3 eggs, organic
- 3 cups bread flour
- 1 cup whole wheat flour
- 3 tablespoons light brown
- 3 teaspoons active dry yeast
- 1 ½ cups water, room temperature
- 5 teaspoons unsalted butter, softened

Directions:
1. Place ingredients in the bread machine pan according to the manufacturer's recommended order.
2. Read the instructions for the bread machine to set the machine's cooking cycle.
3. Select the Basic setting with Medium Crust on your machine, and Start.
4. When the bread is done, take out the bread and let it cool on a cooling rack.
5. Slice after 10 minutes and enjoy!

Nutrition:
Per Serving Calories: 455, Total Fat: 6.2g, Saturated Fat: 3g, Carbohydrates: 82.7g, Fiber: 2.7g, Sodium: 95mg, Protein: 14.7g

Tip: You can substitute butter with coconut oil or olive oil. Plus, the active dry yeast with bread machine yeast in case of availability issues.

9. Peanut Butter Bread

Prep Time: 10 minutes or less
Ready Time: 3 hours 40 minutes

12 Slices/1 ½ pounds
- 3 cups bread flour
- ½ teaspoon fine salt
- ⅓ cup peanut butter
- 4 tablespoons brown sugar
- 2 teaspoons bread machine yeast
- 1 ⅛ cups warm water, 200 degrees F

16 Slices/2 pounds
- 4 cups bread flour
- 1 teaspoon fine salt
- ½ cup peanut butter
- 4 ½ tablespoons brown sugar
- 2 ½ teaspoons bread machine yeast
- 1 ½ cups warm water, 200 degrees F

Directions:
1. Place ingredients in the bread machine pan according to the manufacturer's recommended order.
2. Or simply pour water, peanut butter, yeast, brown sugar, bread flour, and salt into the bread machine.
3. Select the Basic/White bread cycle with Light Crust color, and start.
4. When the bread is done, take out the bread and let it cool on a cooling rack.
5. Slice after 10 minutes and enjoy!

Nutrition:
Per Serving Calories: 508, Total Fat: 11.8g, Saturated Fat: 2.4g, Carbohydrates: 85g, Fiber: 4.2g, Sodium: 397mg, Protein: 15.8g

Tip: You can substitute peanut butter with hazelnut spread if you like and in a shortage. Use only fresh yeast, and to keep it fresh for longer, put it in a Ziploc bag and freeze it until next time.

10. Onion Bread

Prep Time: 25 minutes or less
Ready Time: 2 hours 25 minutes

12 Slices/1 ½ pounds
- A pinch of salt
- 3 cups bread flour
- 1 ½ teaspoons active dry yeast
- 2 tablespoons unsalted butter
- 1 tablespoon brown sugar
- 2 tablespoons nonfat dry milk
- 3 tablespoons dry onion soup mix
- 1 cups water, room temperature

16 Slices/2 pounds
- A pinch of salt
- 4 cups bread flour
- 2 teaspoons active dry yeast
- 3 tablespoons unsalted butter
- 1 ½ tablespoons brown sugar
- 3 tablespoons nonfat dry milk
- 4 tablespoons dry onion soup mix
- 1 ½ cups water, room temperature

Directions:
1. Put all the listed ingredients in the bread pan according to the manufacturer's instructions.
2. Select the Basic Bread or Timed cycle, and start.
3. When you add yeast, make a small cavity in the center of the ingredients, and add it in the center.
4. Add the onion mix when the machine beeps for mix-in ingredients, after around 40 minutes.
5. When the bread is done, take it out carefully and let it cool on a wire rack.
6. Slice after 10 minutes and enjoy!

Nutrition:
Per Serving Calories: 456, Total Fat: 6.8g, Saturated Fat: 3.8g, Carbohydrates: 85g, Fiber: 4.3g, Sodium: 2181mg, Protein: 12.5g

Tip: If you don't have dry milk, you can substitute it with liquid milk.

11. Everyday Half Wheat Bread

Prep Time: 5 minutes or less
Ready Time: 3 hours 5 minutes

12 Slices/1 ½ pounds
- 1 cup water
- 1 teaspoon salt
- 1 teaspoon yeast
- 1 ½ cups whole wheat flour
- 2 tablespoons margarine
- 1 ½ tablespoons molasses/honey
- 1 ½ cups bread flour or all-purpose flour

16 Slices/2 pounds
- 1 ½ cups water
- 1 ½ teaspoons salt
- 1 ½ teaspoons yeast
- 2 cups whole wheat flour
- 2 ½ tablespoons margarine
- 2 tablespoons molasses/honey
- 2 cups bread flour or all-purpose flour

Directions:
1. Place ingredients in the bread machine pan according to the manufacturer's recommended order.
2. Select the Whole Wheat Bread setting, and Start.
3. When the bread is done, take out the pan and let it cool on a cooling rack.
4. Slice after 15 minutes and enjoy!

Nutrition:
Per Serving Calories: 2114, Total Fat: 37.3g, Saturated Fat: 7.4g, Carbohydrates: 396g, Fiber: 34g, Sodium: 3858mg, Protein: 60.3g

Tip: You can substitute honey or molasses with olive oil in case of availability issues.

12. Spelt Everyday Bread

Prep Time: 5 minutes or less
Ready Time: 2 hours 5 minutes

12 Slices/1 ½ pounds
- ½ teaspoon salt
- 3 cups spelt flour
- 1 cup soy milk
- 1 ½ tablespoon canola oil
- 1 ½ tablespoon white sugar
- 2 teaspoons active dry yeast

16 Slices/2 pounds
- 1 teaspoon salt
- 4 cups spelt flour
- 1 ¼ cups soy milk
- 2 tablespoons canola oil
- 2 tablespoons white sugar
- 2 ¼ teaspoons active dry yeast

Directions:
1. Place ingredients in the bread machine pan according to the manufacturer's recommended order.
2. Select the Quick White Bread setting, and Start.
3. When the bread is done, take out the pan and let it cool on a cooling rack.
4. Slice after 10 minutes and enjoy!

Nutrition:
Per Serving Calories: 135, Total Fat: 2.7g, Saturated Fat: 0.3g, Carbohydrates: 24.7g, Fiber: 3.9g, Sodium: 159mg, Protein: 5g

Tip: You can substitute soy milk with rice milk and canola oil with any other neutral oil such as olive oil or grapeseed oil in case of availability issues.

13. Oatmeal Everyday Bread

Prep Time: 5 minutes or less
Ready Time: 3 hours 5 minutes

12 Slices/1 ½ pounds

- 1 ½ cups water
- 1 ½ teaspoons salt
- 2 ½ tablespoons honey
- 3 ⅓ cups bread flour
- ¾ cup quick-cooking oats
- 2 ½ teaspoons active dry yeast
- 2 tablespoons butter, softened

16 Slices/2 pounds

- 2 cups water
- 2 teaspoons salt
- 3 tablespoons honey
- 4 ⅓ cups bread flour
- 1 cup quick-cooking oats
- 3 teaspoons active dry yeast
- 2 ½ tablespoons butter, softened

Directions:

1. Place ingredients in the bread machine pan according to the manufacturer's recommended order.
2. Select the White Bread setting, and Start.
3. When the bread is done, take out the pan and let it cool on a cooling rack.
4. Slice after 10 minutes and enjoy!

Nutrition:

Per Serving Calories: 197, Total Fat: 3g, Saturated Fat: 1.5g, Carbohydrates: 37.2g, Fiber: 1.9g, Sodium: 309mg, Protein: 5.1g

Tip: You can substitute honey with sugar and butter with olive oil or margarine in case of availability issues.

Chapter 4: Whole Wheat Bread Recipes

14. Cocoa Whole Wheat Bread

Prep Time: 5 minutes or less
Ready Time: 3 hours 5 minutes

12 Slices/1 ½ pounds
- 2 eggs, whole
- ½ teaspoon salt
- 1 cup almond milk
- 1/2 cup brown sugar
- 4 tablespoons canola oil
- 3 cups whole wheat flour
- 1 teaspoon vanilla extract
- 1 tablespoon vital wheat gluten
- ½ cup cocoa powder, unsweetened
- 2.5 teaspoons of bread machine yeast

16 Slices/2 pounds
- 3 eggs, whole
- 1 teaspoon salt
- 1 ½ cup almond milk
- 1 cup brown sugar
- 4 ½ tablespoons canola oil
- 4 cups whole wheat flour
- 1 ½ teaspoon vanilla extract
- 1 ½ tablespoon vital wheat gluten
- 1 cup cocoa powder, unsweetened
- 3 teaspoons bread machine yeast

Directions:
1. Place ingredients in the bread machine pan according to the manufacturer's recommended order.
2. Select the Whole Grain bread setting with Medium crust on your machine, and Start.
3. When the bread is done, take out the bread and let it cool on a cooling rack.
4. Slice after 10 minutes and enjoy!

Nutrition:
Per Serving Calories: 482, Total Fat: 21.2g, Saturated Fat: 10.1g, Carbohydrates: 66.5g, Fiber: 5.1g, Sodium: 217mg, Protein: 10.4g

Tip: You can store the bread in a plastic wrap for 1 to 3 days.

15. Cajun Classic Bread

Prep Time: 10 minutes or less
Ready Time: 3 hours 10 minutes

12 Slices/1 ½ pounds
- 1 cup water
- ½ teaspoon salt
- ⅓ cup chopped onion
- 3 cups whole wheat flour
- 1 ½ teaspoons active dry yeast
- 1 ½ teaspoons Cajun seasoning
- 1 ½ tablespoons granulated sugar
- 2 ½ teaspoons finely chopped garlic
- ⅓ cup chopped green bell pepper
- 2 ½ teaspoons unsalted butter, softened and cut into small pieces

16 Slices/2 pounds
- 1 ½ cup water
- 1 teaspoon salt
- ½ cup chopped onion
- 4 cups whole wheat flour
- 2 teaspoons active dry yeast
- 2 teaspoons Cajun seasoning
- 2 tablespoons granulated sugar
- 3 teaspoons finely chopped garlic
- ½ cup chopped green bell pepper
- 3 teaspoons unsalted butter, softened and cut into small pieces

Directions:
1. Place ingredients in the bread machine pan according to the manufacturer's recommended order.
2. Select the Whole Grain bread setting with Dark crust on your machine, and Start.
3. When the bread is done, take out the bread and let it cool on a cooling rack.
4. Slice after 10 minutes and enjoy!

Nutrition:
Per Serving Calories: 298, Total Fat: 4g, Saturated Fat: 1.2g, Carbohydrates: 57.1g, Fiber: 8.5g, Sodium: 175mg, Protein: 10.6g
Tip: We don't recommend using the delay cycle with this recipe.

16. Quinoa & Whole Wheat Bread

Prep Time: 20 minutes or less
Ready Time: 3 hours 50 minutes

12 Slices/1 ½ pounds
- ¾ cup water
- ⅛ teaspoon salt
- 1 ½ cup buttermilk
- 2 teaspoons yeast
- 2 cups bread flour
- 1 cup quinoa flakes
- 1 cup whole-wheat flour
- 1 cup quick-cooking oats
- 2 ½ tablespoons brown sugar
- 8 ½ teaspoons unsalted butter, melted and cooled

16 Slices/2 pounds
- 1 cup water
- ¼ teaspoon salt
- 2 cups buttermilk
- 2 ½ teaspoons yeast
- 2 ½ cups bread flour
- 1 ½ cups quinoa flakes
- 1 ½ cup whole-wheat flour
- 1 ½ cup quick-cooking oats
- 3 tablespoons brown sugar
- 9 teaspoons unsalted butter, melted and cooled

Directions:
1. Cook quinoa in water using a saucepan and boil it for 5 minutes.
2. Then cover and turn off the heat, letting it sit for 10 minutes.
3. Then add quinoa and all the remaining listed ingredients into the bread machine according to the manufacturer's recommended order.
4. Select the Whole Grain cycle on the bread machine, and Start.
5. When the bread is done, take it out and let it cool on a cooling rack.
6. Slice after 10 minutes and enjoy!

Nutrition:

Per Serving Calories: 267, Total Fat: 6.6g, Saturated Fat: 3.6g, Carbohydrates: 43.9g, Fiber: 3.2g, Sodium: 110mg, Protein: 7.8g

Tip: We don't recommend using the delay cycle with this recipe.

17. Whole Wheat Bread with Flaxseed

Prep Time: 10 minutes or less
Ready Time: 3 hours 15 minutes

12 Slices/1 ½ pounds
- 1 teaspoon salt
- 1 cup warm water
- ¼ cups bread flour
- 2 tablespoons honey
- 2 tablespoons olive oil
- 3 cups whole wheat flour
- 4 tablespoons ground flaxseed
- 2-3 teaspoons active dry yeast

16 Slices/2 pounds
- 1 ½ teaspoons salt
- 1 ½ cups warm water
- ⅓ cups bread flour
- 2 ½ tablespoons honey
- 2 ½ tablespoons olive oil
- 3 ½ cups whole wheat flour
- 4 ½ tablespoons ground flaxseed
- 3 teaspoons active dry yeast

Directions:
1. Place ingredients in the bread machine pan according to the manufacturer's recommended order.
2. Or simply pour the warm water, honey, salt, and vegetable oil into the bread machine pan.
3. Then add the whole wheat flour, bread flour, and ground flaxseed.
4. Make a small hole in the center of the flour mixture and add the yeast.
5. Select the Whole Grain setting on the bread machine, and Start.
6. When the bread is done, take it out and cool it onto a cooling rack.
7. Slice after 10 minutes and enjoy!

Nutrition:
Per Serving Calories: 405, Total Fat: 8.4g, Saturated Fat: 0.9g, Carbohydrates: 70.7g, Fiber: 9.3g, Sodium: 392mg, Protein: 13.1g

Tip: Keep a check on your dough during the kneading cycle. If it's too dry, you can add extra water to make the dough soft.

18. Herbed Whole Wheat Bread Recipe

Prep Time: 10 minutes or less
Ready Time: 3 hours 10 minutes

12 Slices/1 ½ pounds
- ½ teaspoon salt
- ½ tablespoon sugar
- 1 ½ tablespoons olive oil
- 2 cloves garlic, crushed
- 3 cups whole wheat flour
- 1 ¼ cups lukewarm water
- 1 ½ tablespoons chopped basil
- ½ teaspoon chopped chives
- 2 teaspoons active dry yeast
- ⅓ teaspoon chopped oregano
- ⅛ teaspoon chopped rosemary
- 3 tablespoons grated Parmesan cheese

16 Slices/2 pounds
- 1 teaspoon salt
- 1 tablespoon sugar
- 2 tablespoons olive oil
- 3 cloves garlic, crushed
- 4 cups whole wheat flour
- 1 ⅓ cups lukewarm water
- 2 tablespoons chopped basil
- 1 teaspoon chopped chives
- 2 ¼ teaspoons active dry yeast
- 1/2 teaspoon chopped oregano
- 1/4 teaspoon chopped rosemary
- 4 tablespoons grated Parmesan cheese

Directions:
1. Place ingredients in the bread machine pan according to the manufacturer's recommended order.

2. Select the Whole Grain bread setting with medium crust on your machine, and Start.
3. When the bread is done, take out the bread and let it cool on a cooling rack.
4. Slice after 10 minutes and enjoy!

Nutrition:
Per Serving Calories: 372, Total Fat: 6.6g, Saturated Fat: 1.5g, Carbohydrates: 66.9g, Fiber: 2.6g, Sodium: 434mg, Protein: 10.7g

Tip: You can increase the amount of herbs or use different types of herbs for an enhanced flavor.

19. Sweet Potato Bread

Prep Time: 15 minutes or less
Ready Time: 2 hours 15 minutes

12 Slices/1 ½ pounds
- 1 ½ tablespoons butter
- ½ teaspoon kosher salt
- ¼ teaspoon cinnamon
- ¼ cup Raisins, optional
- ¼ cup dark brown sugar
- 3 cups whole wheat flour
- ¼ teaspoon vanilla extract
- 1 ½ teaspoons active dry yeast
- ½ cup mashed sweet potatoes
- ¼ teaspoon ground nutmeg
- 1 ½ tablespoons dry milk powder
- ⅓ cup plus 2 tablespoons water
- ¼ cup chopped pecans, optional

16 Slices/2 pounds
- 2 tablespoons butter
- 1 teaspoon kosher salt
- ½ teaspoon cinnamon
- ½ cup Raisins, optional
- ½ cup dark brown sugar
- 4 cups whole wheat flour
- ½ teaspoon vanilla extract
- 2 teaspoons active dry yeast
- 1 cup mashed sweet potatoes
- ½ teaspoon ground nutmeg
- 2 tablespoons dry milk powder
- ½ cup plus 2 tablespoons water

- ½ cup chopped pecans, optional

Directions:
1. Place ingredients in the bread machine pan according to the manufacturer's recommended order.
2. Select the Basic Bread setting with a Light crust on your machine, and Start.
3. Add pecans and raisins when the machine beeps for mix-in ingredients during the ending cycle.
4. When the bread is done, take it out and let it cool on a cooling rack.
5. Slice after 10 minutes and enjoy!

Nutrition:
Per Serving Calories: 459, Total Fat: 4.9g, Saturated Fat: 2.6g, Carbohydrates: 93.9g, Fiber: 3.8g, Sodium: 469mg, Protein: 10.5g

Tip: You can substitute fresh sweet potatoes with canned sweet potatoes in case of availability issues. Though, drain the liquid and rinse the sweet potatoes under water to get rid of extra syrup before using them in the recipe.

20. Black & Green Olive Whole Wheat Bread

Prep Time: 10 minutes or less
Ready Time: 3 hours 10 minutes

12 Slices/1 ½ pounds
- 1 ½ tablespoons honey
- 1 cup warm water
- 1 ½ tablespoons olive oil
- ¼ tablespoon table salt
- 3 cups all-purpose flour
- ½ cup whole wheat flour
- 1 teaspoon dried leaf basil
- 1 teaspoon dried rosemary
- ¼ cup black olives, drained and sliced
- ¼ cup green olives, drained and sliced
- 2 teaspoons bread machine yeast
- ¼ cup reserved juices (brine from green olives)

16 Slices/2 pounds
- 2 tablespoons honey
- 1 ⅓ cups warm water
- 2 tablespoons olive oil
- ½ tablespoon table salt
- 4 cups all-purpose flour
- ⅔ cup whole wheat flour
- 1 ½ teaspoons dried leaf basil
- 1 ½ teaspoons dried rosemary
- ⅓ cup black olives, drained and sliced
- ⅓ cup green olives, drained and sliced
- 2 ¼ teaspoons bread machine yeast (1 packet)
- ⅓ cup reserved juices (brine from green olives)

Directions:
1. Combine the olive brine with warm water.
2. Place all the ingredients except sliced olives in the bread machine pan according to the manufacturer's recommended order.
3. Select the Basic/White Bread cycle with Medium crust, and Start.
4. Once the machine beeps for mix-in ingredients during the final stages, add in the sliced olives.
5. When the bread is done, take it out and let it cool on a cooling rack.
6. Slice after 10 minutes and enjoy!

Nutrition:
Per Serving Calories: 326, Total Fat: 5.8g, Saturated Fat: 0.8g, Carbohydrates: 60.4g, Fiber: 3.6g, Sodium: 277mg, Protein: 8.4g

Tip: If your dough is too sticky, you can add more flour. The same is true for water if your dough is too stiff.

21. Sesame Whole Wheat Bread

Prep Time: 5 minutes or less
Ready Time: 3 hours 5 minutes

12 Slices/1 ½ pounds
- A few pinches salt
- ¼ cup maple syrup
- ¼ cup sesame seeds
- 2 tablespoons olive oil
- 1 ¼ cups lukewarm water
- 2 teaspoons instant yeast
- 3 ½ cups Whole Wheat Flour
- 1 tablespoon vital wheat gluten

16 Slices/2 pounds
- A few pinches salt
- ⅓ cup maple syrup
- ⅓ cup sesame seeds
- 2 ½ tablespoons olive oil
- 1 ⅓ cups lukewarm water
- 2 ½ teaspoons instant yeast
- 4 cups Whole Wheat Flour
- 1 ½ tablespoon vital wheat gluten

Directions:
1. Place all the ingredients in the bread machine pan according to the manufacturer's recommended order.
2. Select the Whole Wheat Bread cycle (if available) or simply Basic White bread, and Start.
3. When the bread is done, take it out and let it cool on a cooling rack.
4. Slice after 10 minutes and enjoy!

Nutrition:
Per Serving Calories: 576, Total Fat: 12.7g, Saturated Fat: 1.8g, Carbohydrates: 100.3g, Fiber: 4.4g, Sodium: 6mg, Protein: 14.9g

Tip: Keep an eye on the dough in the kneading cycle especially after 10 to 12 minutes of kneading. Your dough should be smooth, not lumpy or sticky, for the bread to turn out perfect.

22. Whole Wheat Cinnamon Raisin Bread

Prep Time: 10 minutes or less
Ready Time: 4 hours 5 minutes

12 Slices/1 ½ pounds
- ½ cup raisins
- 1 cup warm water
- 1 ½ teaspoons salt
- 2 tablespoons honey
- 1 ½ cups bread flour
- 2 tablespoons vegetable oil
- 1 ½ cups whole wheat flour
- 2 teaspoons active dry yeast
- 2 teaspoons ground cinnamon

16 Slices/2 pounds
- 1 cup raisins
- 1 ½ cup warm water
- 2 teaspoons salt
- 2 ½ tablespoons honey
- 2 cups bread flour
- 2 ½ tablespoons vegetable oil
- 2 cups whole wheat flour
- 2 ½ teaspoons active dry yeast
- 2 ½ teaspoons ground cinnamon

Directions:
1. Place ingredients in the bread machine pan according to the manufacturer's recommended order.
2. Or simply pour warm water, honey, vegetable oil, and salt into the bread machine pan.
3. Add whole wheat flour on top of it along with bread flour, ground cinnamon, and raisins.
4. Make a small hole in the center of this mixture and add the yeast.
5. Select the Whole Wheat setting on your bread machine, and Start.
6. When the bread is done, take it out and let it cool on a cooling rack.
7. Slice after 10 minutes and serve.

Nutrition:
Per Serving Calories: 394, Total Fat: 6g, Saturated Fat: 1.2g, Carbohydrates: 75g, Fiber: 2.4g, Sodium: 703mg, Protein: 9.8g

23. Whole Wheat Bread with Sunflower Seed

Prep Time: 5 minutes or less
Ready Time: 3 hours 5 minutes

12 Slices/1 ½ pounds
- A pinch of salt
- 1 cup warm water
- 2 tablespoons honey
- 1 ½ cups wheat flour
- ⅓ cup sunflower seeds
- 2 tablespoons vegetable oil
- 2 teaspoons active dry yeast
- 1 ½ cups whole grain wheat flour

16 Slices/2 pounds
- ⅛ teaspoon salt
- 1 ½ cups warm water
- 2 ½ tablespoons honey
- 2 cups wheat flour
- ½ cup sunflower seeds
- 2 ½ tablespoons vegetable oil
- 2 ½ teaspoons active dry yeast
- 2 cups whole grain wheat flour

Directions:
1. Place ingredients in the bread machine pan according to the manufacturer's recommended order.
2. Or simply put warm water, oil, honey, and salt into the bread machine pan.
3. Top it with whole wheat flour, bread flour, and sunflower seeds.
4. Create a small well in the center of the flour and add the yeast.
5. Select the Whole Wheat setting on your bread machine.
6. When the bread is done, take it out and let it cool on a cooling rack.
7. Slice after 10 minutes and enjoy!

Nutrition:
Per Serving Calories: 450, Total Fat: 10.2g, Saturated Fat: 1.7g, Carbohydrates: 75g, Fiber: 7.8g, Sodium: 46mg, Protein: 12.9g
Tip: Serve the bread with a nice jam or butter.

24. Simple Whole Wheat Bread

Prep Time: 5 minutes or less
Ready Time: 3 hours 5 minutes

12 Slices/1 ½ pounds
- 2 eggs
- 1 ½ teaspoon salt
- 2 cups bread flour
- ½ cup warm milk
- ½ cup warm water
- 3 tablespoons honey
- 1 cup whole wheat flour
- 2 tablespoons butter, softened
- 2 ¼ teaspoons active dry yeast

16 Slices/2 pounds
- 3 egg
- 2 teaspoons salt
- 2 ½ cups bread flour
- 1 cup warm milk
- 1 cup warm water
- 3 ½ tablespoons honey
- 1 ½ cups whole wheat flour
- 2 ½ tablespoons butter, softened
- 2 ½ teaspoons active dry yeast

Directions:
1. Place ingredients in the bread machine pan according to the manufacturer's recommended order.
2. Select Basic Bread setting on the bread machine with crust and loaf size of your choice, and Start.
3. When the bread is done, take it out and let it cool on a cooling rack.
4. Slice after 10 minutes and enjoy!

Nutrition:
Per Serving Calories: 159, Total Fat: 2.8g, Saturated Fat: 1.5g, Carbohydrates: 29g, Fiber: 1g, Sodium: 316mg, Protein: 4.4g

Tip: We don't recommend using the delay cycle with this recipe.

25. Whole Grain Seed Loaf

Prep Time: 20 minutes or less
Ready Time: 4 hours 20 minutes

12 Slices/1 ½ pounds
- 1 ¼ teaspoons salt
- 1 tablespoon millet
- 3 tablespoons honey
- 1 tablespoon flaxseed
- 1 ⅓ cups 2% warm milk
- 2 tablespoons canola oil
- 1 tablespoon cracked wheat
- 2 ⅔ cups whole wheat flour
- 4 teaspoons vital wheat gluten
- 1 tablespoon sunflower kernels
- 2 ½ teaspoons active dry yeast
- 2 tablespoons old fashioned oats

16 Slices/2 pounds
- 1 ½ teaspoons salt
- 1 ½ tablespoons millet
- 3 ½ tablespoons honey
- 1 ½ tablespoons flaxseed
- 1 ½ cups 2% warm milk
- 2 ½ tablespoons canola oil
- 1 ½ tablespoons cracked wheat
- 3 cups whole wheat flour
- 4 ½ teaspoons vital wheat gluten
- 1 ½ tablespoon sunflower kernels
- 2 ¾ teaspoons active dry yeast
- 2 ½ tablespoons old fashioned oats

Directions:
1. Place ingredients in the bread machine pan according to the manufacturer's recommended order.
2. Select Basic Bread setting on the bread machine with crust and loaf size of your choice, and Start.
3. When the bread is done, take it out and let it cool on a cooling rack.
4. Slice after 10 minutes and enjoy!

Nutrition:
Per Serving Calories: 128, Total Fat: 3g, Saturated Fat: 1g, Carbohydrates: 21g, Fiber: 3g, Sodium: 199mg, Protein: 5g

26. Whole Wheat Banana Bread

Prep Time: 15 minutes or less
Ready Time: 4 hours 15 minutes

12 Slices/1 ½ pounds
- ¼ cup honey
- 1 teaspoon salt
- ¾ cup warm water
- 1 ¾ cups bread flour
- 4 ½ teaspoons canola oil
- 2 teaspoons poppy seeds
- ½ teaspoon vanilla extract
- 1 ½ cups whole wheat flour
- 1 medium ripe banana, sliced
- 2 ¼ teaspoons active dry yeast
- 1 large egg, lightly beaten, room temperature

16 Slices/2 pounds
- ⅓ cup honey
- 1 ½ teaspoons salt
- 1 cup warm water
- 2 cups bread flour
- 5 teaspoons canola oil
- 2 ½ teaspoons poppy seeds
- 1 teaspoon vanilla extract
- 2 cups whole wheat flour
- 1 large ripe banana, sliced
- 2 ½ teaspoons active dry yeast
- 2 eggs, lightly beaten, room temperature

Directions:
1. Place ingredients in the bread machine pan according to the manufacturer's recommended order.
2. Select Basic Bread setting on the bread machine with crust and loaf size of your choice, and Start.
3. When the bread is done, take it out and let it cool on a cooling rack.
4. Slice after 10 minutes and enjoy!

Nutrition:
Per Serving Calories: 125, Total Fat: 2g, Saturated Fat: 0g, Carbohydrates: 24g, Fiber: 2g, Sodium: 153mg, Protein: 4g

Chapter 5: Breakfast Bread Recipes

27. French Bread with A Crust

Prep Time: 15 minutes or less
Ready Time: 3 hours 55 minutes

12 Slices/1 ½ pounds
- 1 ½ teaspoons salt
- 2 small egg whites
- 1 ½ cups bread flour
- 1 ½ teaspoons sugar
- 1 ½ tablespoons dry milk
- 1 ½ cups all-purpose flour
- ½ tablespoon cold water
- ½ tablespoon vegetable oil
- 1 ½ teaspoons active dry yeast
- 1 cup water, room temperature
- 1 ½ tablespoons medium-grind cornmeal

16 Slices/2 pounds
- 2 teaspoons salt
- 3 small egg whites
- 2 cups bread flour
- 2 teaspoons sugar
- 2 tablespoons dry milk
- 2 cups all-purpose flour
- 1 tablespoon cold water
- 1 tablespoon vegetable oil
- 2 teaspoons active dry yeast
- 1 ½ cups water, room temperature
- 2 tablespoons medium-grind cornmeal

Directions:
1. Place ingredients in the bread machine pan according to the manufacturer's recommended order.
2. Select the French Bread Cycle on your bread machine, and press Start.
3. When the bread is done, unplug the machine and remove the pan.
4. Gently shake the bucket to remove the bread, and place it on a cooling rack.
5. Slice after 10 minutes and enjoy!

Nutrition:
Per Serving Calories: 186, Total Fat: 2g, Saturated Fat: 0g, Carbohydrates: 35g, Fiber: 1g, Sodium: 365mg, Protein: 6g

Tip: To ensure the bread is fully cooked from inside, insert a quick-read thermometer inside the center of the loaf and if it reads between 195 - 200 F, your bread is done.

28. Bran Bread with Oat

Prep Time: 10 minutes or less
Ready Time: 3 hours 15 minutes

12 Slices/1 ½ pounds
- ¼ cup oat bran
- 1 teaspoon salt
- 2 tablespoons honey
- 2 ½ cups bread flour
- 1 ¼ cups warm water
- 2 tablespoons margarine
- 1 ½ teaspoon active dry yeast

16 Slices/2 pounds
- ⅓ cup oat bran
- 1 ½ teaspoons salt
- 2 ½ tablespoons honey
- 3 cups bread flour
- 1 ½ cups warm water
- 2 ½ tablespoons margarine
- 2 teaspoons active dry yeast

Directions:
1. Place ingredients in the bread machine pan according to the manufacturer's recommended order.
2. Select the Basic/White Bread Cycle on your bread machine, and press Start.
3. When the bread is done, unplug the machine and remove the pan.
4. Gently shake the bucket to remove the bread, and place it on a cooling rack.
5. Slice after 10 minutes and enjoy!

Nutrition:
Per Serving Calories: 136, Total Fat: 2g, Saturated Fat: 0g, Carbohydrates: 25g, Fiber: 1g, Sodium: 216mg, Protein: 4g

Tip: You can substitute honey with brown sugar and margarine with butter or vegetable oil in case of availability issues.

29. Tomato & Olive Bread

Prep Time: 20 minutes or less
Ready Time: 20 minutes

12 Slices/1 ½ pounds
- ½ teaspoon salt
- 2 ¾ cups bread flour
- 2 tablespoons olive oil
- 1 cup warm tomato juice
- 2 teaspoons brown sugar
- 2 ¼ teaspoons quick-rise yeast
- 1 tablespoon fresh minced or dried rosemary
- ½ cup chopped pitted green olives, drained well
- ½ cup chopped oil-packed sun-dried tomatoes, drained well

16 Slices/2 pounds
- 1 teaspoon salt
- 3 ¾ cups bread flour
- 2 ½ tablespoons olive oil
- 1 ½ cups warm tomato juice
- 2 ½ teaspoons brown sugar
- 2 ½ teaspoons quick-rise yeast
- 1 ½ tablespoons fresh minced or dried rosemary
- 1 cup chopped pitted green olives, drained well
- 1 cup chopped oil-packed sun-dried tomatoes, drained well

Directions:
1. Place ingredients except tomatoes and olives in the bread machine pan according to the manufacturer's recommended order.
2. When the machine beeps for mix-in ingredients some time before the kneading cycle ends, add in the tomatoes and the olives.
3. Select the Basic/White Bread Cycle with Medium Crust on your bread machine, and press Start.
4. When the bread is done, unplug the machine and remove the pan.
5. Gently shake the bucket to remove the bread, and place it on a cooling rack.
6. Slice after 10 minutes and enjoy!

Nutrition:
Per Serving Calories: 126, Total Fat: 4g, Saturated Fat: 1g, Carbohydrates: 20g, Fiber: 1g, Sodium: 194mg, Protein: 3g

Tip: Serve the bread with extra-virgin olive oil. Dip pieces of the bread in and enjoy the exquisite flavor.

30. Amish White Bread Loaf

Prep Time: 5 minutes or less
Ready Time: 4 hours 55 minutes

12 Slices/1 ½ pounds
- ¼ cup canola oil
- ½ teaspoon salt
- ¼ cup white sugar
- 2 ¾ cups bread flour
- 1 ⅛ cups warm water
- 1 teaspoon active dry yeast

16 Slices/2 pounds
- ½ cup canola oil
- 1 teaspoon salt
- ½ cup white sugar
- 3 ¾ cups bread flour
- 1 ¼ cups warm water
- 1 ½ teaspoons active dry yeast

Directions:
1. Place ingredients in the bread machine pan according to the manufacturer's recommended order.
2. Select the White Bread Cycle on your bread machine, and press Start.
3. When the bread is done, unplug the machine and remove the pan.
4. Gently shake the bucket to remove the bread, and place it on a cooling rack.

5. Slice after 10 minutes and enjoy!

Nutrition:
Per Serving Calories: 58, Total Fat: 5g, Saturated Fat: 0g, Carbohydrates: 4g, Fiber: 0g, Sodium: 98mg, Protein: 0g

Tip: Only use bread flour with this recipe for the best results. Also, if you like an enhanced flavor, adding 1 to 2 teaspoons of cinnamon would do the trick.

31. Lightweight Oat Bread

Prep Time: 5 minutes or less
Ready Time: 3 hours 55 minutes

12 Slices/1 ½ pounds
- 1 ¼ cups water
- 1 teaspoon salt
- ½ cup rolled oats
- 3 cups all-purpose flour
- 2 tablespoons margarine
- 2 tablespoons brown sugar
- 1 ½ teaspoons active dry yeast

16 Slices/2 pounds
- 1 ½ cups water
- 1 ½ teaspoons salt
- 1 cup rolled oats
- 4 cups all-purpose flour
- 2 ½ tablespoons margarine
- 2 ½ tablespoons brown sugar
- 2 teaspoons active dry yeast

Directions:
1. Place ingredients in the bread machine pan according to the manufacturer's recommended order.
2. Select the Regular Bread cycle with Light crust on your bread machine, and press Start.
3. When the bread is done, unplug the machine and remove the pan.
4. Gently shake the bucket to remove the bread, and place it on a cooling rack.
5. Slice after 10 minutes and enjoy!

Nutrition:
Per Serving Calories: 152, Total Fat: 2g, Saturated Fat: 0g, Carbohydrates: 29g, Fiber: 0g, Sodium: 216mg, Protein: 4g

Tip: You can increase the amount of oats for personal preference but make sure the dough remains soft, not stiff at all.

32. Whole Grain Wheat Bread

Prep Time: 10 minutes or less
Ready Time: 3 hours 10 minutes

12 Slices/1 ½ pounds
- ⅓ cup honey
- 1 teaspoon salt
- 1 ½ cups bread flour
- 1 cup warm water
- 1 ½ cups whole wheat flour
- 1 ½ tablespoons white sugar
- 1 ½ tablespoons butter, softened
- 1 ½ teaspoons instant coffee granules
- 1 ½ teaspoons bread machine yeast
- 1 ½ tablespoons unsweetened cocoa powder

16 Slices/2 pounds
- ½ cup honey
- 1 ½ teaspoons salt
- 2 cups bread flour
- 1 ½ cup warm water
- 2 cups whole wheat flour
- 2 tablespoons white sugar
- 2 tablespoons butter, softened
- 2 teaspoons instant coffee granules
- 2 teaspoons bread machine yeast
- 2 tablespoons unsweetened cocoa powder

Directions:
1. Place ingredients in the bread machine pan according to the manufacturer's recommended order.
2. Select the Regular or Basic Bread cycle with Light crust on your bread machine, and press Start.
3. When the bread is done, unplug the machine and remove the pan.
4. Gently shake the bucket to remove the bread, and place it on a cooling rack.
5. Slice after 10 minutes and enjoy!

Nutrition:
Per Serving Calories: 167, Total Fat: 2g, Saturated Fat: 1g, Carbohydrates: 34g, Fiber: 3g, Sodium: 158mg, Protein: 5g

Tip: You can replace honey with molasses if you prefer a slightly less sweet flavor or are facing availability issues.

33. Soft Everyday Bread

Prep Time: 10 minutes or less
Ready Time: 3 hours 15 minutes

12 Slices/1 ½ pounds
- 1 teaspoon salt
- 1 ½ cups warm water
- 4 ½ teaspoons honey
- 4 ½ teaspoons olive oil
- 3 cups all-purpose flour
- 2 ½ teaspoons active dry yeast

16 Slices/2 pounds
- 1 ½ teaspoons salt
- 2 cups warm water
- 5 teaspoons honey
- 5 teaspoons olive oil
- 4 cups all-purpose flour
- 3 teaspoons active dry yeast

Directions:
1. Place ingredients in the bread machine pan according to the manufacturer's recommended order.
2. Or simply put warm water in the pan of the bread machine and mix in honey until it dissolves.
3. Next mix in yeast and let it rest for 10 minutes or until foamy.
4. Add the remaining ingredients according to the manufacturer's recommended order.
5. Select Soft cycle if available, or Regular setting, and Start.
6. When the bread is done, take it out and let it cool on a cooling rack.
7. Slice after 25 minutes and enjoy!

Nutrition:
Per Serving Calories: 149, Total Fat: 3g, Saturated Fat: 0g, Carbohydrates: 27g, Fiber: 1g, Sodium: 148mg, Protein: 4g

Tip: Always cool down the bread before slicing for neater cuts.

34. Caraway Rye Bread Loaf

Prep Time: 10 minutes or less
Ready Time: 4 hours 10 minutes

12 Slices/1 ½ pounds
- ½ teaspoon salt
- ⅔ cup rye flour
- 1 ½ tablespoons butter
- 1 ⅔ cups bread flour
- 1 ½ tablespoons molasses
- ⅔ cup whole wheat flour
- 1 ⅛ cups lukewarm water
- 1 ½ tablespoons brown sugar
- 1 tablespoons caraway seeds
- 1 ½ teaspoons active dry yeast
- 1 ½ tablespoons dry milk powder

16 Slices/2 pounds
- 1 teaspoon salt
- ¾ cup rye flour
- 2 tablespoons butter
- 1 ¾ cups bread flour
- 2 tablespoons molasses
- ¾ cup whole wheat flour
- 1 ¼ cups lukewarm water
- 2 tablespoons brown sugar
- 1 ½ tablespoons caraway seeds
- 1 ¾ teaspoons active dry yeast
- 2 tablespoons dry milk powder

Directions:
1. Place ingredients in the bread machine pan according to the manufacturer's recommended order.
2. Select the Grain cycle with crust and loaf size of your choice, and press Start.
3. When the bread is done, unplug the machine and remove the pan.

4. Gently shake the bucket to remove the bread, and place it on a cooling rack.
5. Slice after 10 minutes and enjoy!

Nutrition:
Per Serving Calories: 93, Total Fat: 2g, Saturated Fat: 1g, Carbohydrates: 17g, Fiber: 2g, Sodium: 218mg, Protein: 2g

Tip: If you are low on caraway seeds, you can add in fennel seeds instead.

35. Simple Breakfast Milk Bread

Prep Time: 5 minutes or less
Ready Time: 2 hours

12 Slices/1 ½ pounds
- 1 ⅛ cups milk
- 1 teaspoon salt
- 3 cups all-purpose flour
- 3 tablespoons white sugar
- 1 ½ teaspoons active dry yeast

16 Slices/2 pounds
- 1 ¼ cups milk
- 1 ½ teaspoons salt
- 4 cups all-purpose flour
- 3 ½ tablespoons white sugar
- 2 teaspoons active dry yeast

Directions:
1. Place ingredients in the bread machine pan according to the manufacturer's recommended order.
2. Select the Regular/White Bread cycle, and press Start.
3. When the bread is done, unplug the machine and remove the pan.
4. Gently shake the bucket to remove the bread, and place it on a cooling rack.
5. Slice after 10 minutes and enjoy!

Nutrition:
Per Serving Calories: 111, Total Fat: 1g, Saturated Fat: 0g, Carbohydrates: 23g, Fiber: 1g, Sodium: 163mg, Protein: 3g

Tip: If the dough feels too stiff during the kneading cycle, you can add a little oil and more milk. You can substitute regular milk with soy milk for a vegan approach and in case of availability issues.

36. Potato Crust Bread Loaf

Prep Time: 5 minutes or less
Ready Time: 3 hours 5 minutes

12 Slices/1 ½ pounds
- 1 ¼ cups water
- 1 ½ teaspoons salt
- 3 ¼ cups bread flour
- 2 tablespoons butter
- 1 tablespoon white sugar
- 2 teaspoons instant yeast
- ½ cup instant mashed potato flakes

16 Slices/2 pounds
- 1 ⅓ cups water
- 2 teaspoons salt
- 4 ¼ cups bread flour
- 2 ½ tablespoons butter
- 1 ½ tablespoon white sugar
- 2 ½ teaspoons instant yeast
- 1 cup instant mashed potato flakes

Directions:
1. Place ingredients in the bread machine pan according to the manufacturer's recommended order.
2. Select the White Bread cycle, and press Start.
3. When the bread is done, unplug the machine and remove the pan.
4. Gently shake the bucket to remove the bread, and place it on a cooling rack.
5. Slice after 10 minutes and enjoy!

Nutrition:
Per Serving Calories: 24, Total Fat: 2g, Saturated Fat: 0g, Carbohydrates: 2g, Fiber: 1g, Sodium: 245mg, Protein: 0g

Tip: You can add a tablespoon of rosemary to enhance the flavor of the bread.

37. Breakfast Cranberry & Orange Bread

Prep Time: 5 minutes or less
Ready Time: 3 hours 5 minutes

12 Slices/1 ½ pounds
- 1 teaspoon salt
- 3 cups bread flour
- 2 tablespoons honey
- 1 ⅛ cups orange juice
- ⅓ cup chopped walnuts
- 2 tablespoons vegetable oil
- ½ teaspoon ground allspice
- 1 tablespoon dry milk powder
- ½ teaspoon ground cinnamon
- 2 ¼ teaspoons active dry yeast
- 1 tablespoon grated orange zest
- 1 cup sweetened dried cranberries

16 Slices/2 pounds
- 1 ½ teaspoons salt
- 4 cups bread flour
- 2 ½ tablespoons honey
- 1 ¼ cups orange juice
- ½ cup chopped walnuts
- 2 ½ tablespoons vegetable oil
- 1 teaspoon ground allspice
- 1 ½ tablespoon dry milk powder
- 1 teaspoon ground cinnamon
- 2 ½ teaspoons active dry yeast
- 1 ½ tablespoons grated orange zest
- 1 ½ cups sweetened dried cranberries

Directions:
1. Place ingredients in the bread machine pan according to the manufacturer's recommended order.
2. Select the Regular cycle, and press Start.
3. Add the dried cranberries and walnuts when the bread machine signals for mix-in ingredients.
4. When the bread is done, unplug the machine and remove the pan.
5. Gently shake the bucket to remove the bread, and place it on a cooling rack.
6. Slice after 10 minutes and enjoy!

Nutrition:

Per Serving Calories: 224, Total Fat: 5g, Saturated Fat: 1g, Carbohydrates: 40g, Fiber: 2g, Sodium: 199mg, Protein: 5g

Tip: You can increase the amount of cranberries and walnuts if you would like a stronger flavor.

38. Flaxseed Whole Wheat Bread

Prep Time: 5 minutes or less
Ready Time: 4 hours 5 minutes

12 Slices/1 ½ pounds
- ⅓ cup honey
- 1 ½ teaspoons salt
- 1 ⅔ cups water
- 1 ½ cups bread flour
- ⅓ cup ground flax seed
- 2 ½ teaspoons active dry yeast
- 1 ½ cups whole wheat flour
- 2 tablespoons vegetable oil
- 1 ½ tablespoon vital wheat gluten
- 2 ½ tablespoons dry milk powder

16 Slices/2 pounds
- ½ cup honey
- 2 teaspoons salt
- 1 ¾ cups water
- 2 cups bread flour
- ½ cup ground flax seed
- 3 teaspoons active dry yeast
- 2 cups whole wheat flour
- 2 ½ tablespoons vegetable oil
- 2 tablespoon vital wheat gluten
- 3 tablespoons dry milk powder

Directions:
1. Place ingredients in the bread machine pan according to the manufacturer's recommended order.
2. Select the Whole Wheat Bread cycle, and press Start.
3. When the bread is done, unplug the machine and remove the pan.
4. Gently shake the bucket to remove the bread, and place it on a cooling rack.
5. Slice after 10 minutes and enjoy!

Nutrition:
Per Serving Calories: 168, Total Fat: 7g, Saturated Fat: 1g, Carbohydrates: 23g, Fiber: 5g, Sodium: 245mg, Protein: 6g

Tip: You can decrease the amount of flaxseed if you don't prefer their taste and crunchiness.

39. Sunflower Seed Bran Bread

Prep Time: 10 minutes or less
Ready Time: 3 hours 10 minutes

12 Slices/1 ½ pounds
- 3 cups bread flour
- ½ cup wheat bran
- 1 teaspoon white sugar
- ¼ cup sunflower seeds
- 3 tablespoons molasses
- 1 ¼ cups warm skim milk
- 2 teaspoons active dry yeast
- 2 tablespoons margarine, melted

16 Slices/2 pounds
- 4 cups bread flour
- 1 cup wheat bran
- 1 ½ teaspoons white sugar
- ½ cup sunflower seeds
- 3 ½ tablespoons molasses
- 1 ½ cups warm skim milk
- 2 ½ teaspoons active dry yeast
- 2 ½ tablespoons margarine, melted

Directions:
1. Place ingredients in the bread machine pan according to the manufacturer's recommended order.
2. Select the appropriate cycle, and press Start.
3. Add sunflower seeds when the machine beeps for mix-in ingredients.
4. When the bread is done, unplug the machine and remove the pan.
5. Gently shake the bucket to remove the bread, and place it on a cooling rack.
6. Slice after 10 minutes and enjoy!

Nutrition:
Per Serving Calories: 97, Total Fat: 5g, Saturated Fat: 1g, Carbohydrates: 12g, Fiber: 2g, Sodium: 51mg, Protein: 3g

Tip: You can increase the quantity of sunflower seeds if you prefer a stronger taste. You can also replace some of the bread flour with whole wheat for enhancing the taste and if you are low on the bread flour.

Chapter 6: Spice, Herb & Vegetable Bread Recipes

40. Garlic Herb Bread

Prep Time: 10 minutes or less
Ready Time: 2 hours 10 minutes

12 Slices/1 ½ pounds

- 1 ½ teaspoons salt
- 3 cups white flour
- 1 cup 1% milk, warm
- 1 tablespoon light butter
- 1 tablespoon white sugar
- 3 teaspoons garlic powder
- 2 teaspoons active dry yeast
- 1 ½ teaspoons Italian seasoning or basil

16 Slices/2 pounds

- 2 teaspoons salt
- 4 cups white flour
- 1 ½ - 2 cup 1% milk, warm
- 2 tablespoon light butter
- 1 ½ tablespoon white sugar
- 3 ½ teaspoons garlic powder
- 2 ½ teaspoons active dry yeast
- 2 teaspoons Italian seasoning or basil

Directions:

1. Place ingredients in the bread machine pan according to the manufacturer's recommended order.
2. Select the Basic Bread Cycle/White on your bread machine, and press Start.

3. The wet ingredients are usually added first to the bottom of the pan, followed with the dry ingredients to cover the wet ingredients.
4. Add a sprinkling of yeast at last, on the top.
5. When the bread is done, unplug the machine and remove the pan.
6. Gently shake the bucket to remove the bread, and place it on a cooling rack.
7. Slice after 10 minutes and enjoy!

Nutrition:

Per Serving Calories: 346, Total Fat: 8g, Saturated Fat: 1g, Carbohydrates: 55g, Fiber: 1g, Sodium: 585mg, Protein: 7g

Tip: You can substitute milk for dry milk and dry active yeast for bread yeast in case of availability issues.

41. Italian Herb & Cheese Bread

Prep Time: 10 minutes or less
Ready Time: 3 hours 10 minutes

12 Slices/1 ½ pounds

- 1 ¼ cup water
- 1 teaspoon salt
- 2 teaspoons sugar
- 3 ½ cups bread flour
- ½ teaspoon dried basil
- 1 ½ tablespoons olive oil
- 2 teaspoons active dry yeast
- 2 teaspoons dried onion flakes
- ¼ cup grated parmesan cheese
- 1 tablespoon dried parsley flakes
- ½ teaspoon garlic powder or 1 teaspoon dried garlic flakes

16 Slices/2 pounds

- 1 ½ cup water
- 2 teaspoons salt
- 3 teaspoons sugar
- 4 cups bread flour
- 1 teaspoon dried basil
- 2 tablespoons olive oil
- 3 teaspoons active dry yeast
- 2 teaspoons dried onion flakes
- ½ cup grated parmesan cheese
- 2 tablespoons dried parsley flakes
- 1 teaspoon garlic powder or 2 teaspoons dried garlic flakes

Directions:

1. Place ingredients in the bread machine pan according to the manufacturer's recommended order.
2. Or, add wet ingredients first to the bottom of the pan, followed with the dry ingredients except yeast to cover the wet ingredients.
3. Create a well in the dry ingredients and add the yeast in it.
4. Select the French Bread setting on your bread machine with the Crust setting of choice, and press Start.
5. When the bread is done, unplug the machine and remove the pan.
6. Let it rest for 5 minutes.
7. Gently remove the bread from the pan, and place it on a cooling rack.
8. Slice after 10 minutes and enjoy!

Nutrition:
Per Serving Calories: 1956, Total Fat: 32.4g, Saturated Fat: 7.9g, Carbohydrates: 350g, Fiber: 14.9g, Sodium: 2738mg, Protein: 59g

Tip: French Bread setting takes longer than Basic Bread/White setting. So, plan accordingly for dinner preparation. Make sure the ingredients are at room temperature.

42. Potato Whole Wheat Bread

Prep Time: 10 minutes or less
Ready Time: 3 hours 10 minutes

12 Slices/1 ½ pounds
- 1 cup bread flour
- 1 ½ teaspoon salt
- 2 cups whole wheat flour
- 1 ½ teaspoons active dry yeast
- 3 tablespoons granulated sugar
- ½ cup dry instant potato flakes
- 1 ⅛ cups warm water, 90 degrees
- 4 tablespoons butter/margarine, softened and cubed

16 Slices/2 pounds
- 2 cups bread flour
- 2 teaspoons salt
- 3 cups whole wheat flour

- 2 teaspoons active dry yeast
- 4 tablespoons granulated sugar
- 1 cup dry instant potato flakes
- 2 cups warm water, 90 degrees
- 5 tablespoons butter/margarine, softened and cubed

Directions:

1. Place ingredients in the bread machine pan according to the manufacturer's recommended order.
2. Select the Basic Bread/Light Crust Cycle on your bread machine, and press Start.
3. When the bread is done, unplug the machine and remove the pan.
4. Let it rest for 5 minutes.
5. Gently remove the bread from the pan and place it on a cooling rack.

Nutrition:
Per Serving Calories: 153, Total Fat: 4.5g, Saturated Fat: 2.5g, Carbohydrates: 26.7g, Fiber: 2.6g, Sodium: 327mg, Protein: 4.1g

Tip: You can use the delay timer with this bread recipe.

43. Kalamata Olive Oil Bread

Prep Time: 10 minutes or less
Ready Time: 2 hours 10 minutes

12 Slices/1 ½ pounds
- ½ cup water
- 2 ½ cups bread flour
- 1 teaspoon salt
- 2 tablespoon sugar
- ⅓ cup olive brine
- 2 tablespoons olive oil
- 1 teaspoon dried basil
- ½ cup whole wheat flour
- 2 teaspoons dry active yeast
- ½ cup Kalamata Olives, finely-chopped

16 Slices/2 pounds
- 1 cup water
- 3 cups bread flour
- 1 ½ teaspoons salt

- 2 tablespoons sugar
- ⅓ - ½ cup olive brine
- 2 tablespoons olive oil
- 1 ½ teaspoons dried basil
- 1 ⅔ cups whole wheat flour
- 2 teaspoons dry active yeast
- ½ - ⅔ cup Kalamata Olives, finely-chopped

Directions:
1. Assemble the ingredients and place them in the pan except for the olives according to the manufacturer's recommended order.
2. Select the Basic/White setting on your machine.
3. Once the machine beeps for mix-in ingredients, place in the olives.
4. Once the loaf is done, remove the pan and let it cool on a cooling rack.
5. Slice after 10 minutes and enjoy!

Nutrition:
Per Serving Calories: 272, Total Fat: 6g, Saturated Fat: 1g, Carbohydrates: 48g, Fiber: 4g, Sodium: 394mg, Protein: 8g

Tip: Add ⅓ cup olive brine in a 2 cup measure and add warm water to make ½ cup total liquid. This will enhance the bread's olive flavor. You can experiment with different herbs for your preferred aromatic taste. Plus, can even substitute Kalamata Olives for Green Olives for an enhanced olive taste.

44. Star Anise Seed Bread

Prep Time: 10 minutes or less
Ready Time: 3 hours 10 minutes

12 Slices/1 ½ pounds
- 1 cup milk
- ¼ cup water
- 1 egg, whisked
- 1 teaspoon salt
- ⅓ cup white sugar
- 2 ½ cups bread flour
- 1 teaspoon anise seeds
- 1 ½ cups yellow corn flour
- 2 ½ teaspoons active dry yeast

- 3 tablespoons butter/margarine, softened

16 Slices/2 pounds
- 1 ½ cups milk
- 1 cup water
- 2 eggs, whisked
- 1 ½ teaspoons salt
- ½ cup white sugar
- 3 cups bread flour
- 1 ½ teaspoon anise seeds
- 2 cups yellow corn flour
- 3 teaspoons active dry yeast
- 4 tablespoons butter/margarine, softened

Directions:
1. Place ingredients in the bread machine pan according to the manufacturer's recommended order.
2. Select the White Bread Cycle on your bread machine, and press Start.
3. When the bread is done, unplug the machine and remove the pan.
4. Let it rest for 5 minutes.
5. Gently remove the bread from the pan and place it on a cooling rack.
6. Slice after 10 minutes and enjoy!

Nutrition:
Per Serving Calories: 214, Total Fat: 4.5g, Saturated Fat: 1g, Carbohydrates: 38.2g, Fiber: 2.9g, Sodium: 243mg, Protein: 5.2g

Tip: Make sure the ingredients are at room temperature.

45. Orange Spice Bread

Prep Time: 10 minutes or less
Ready Time: 10 minutes

12 Slices/1 ½ pounds
- 2 eggs
- ⅔ cup milk
- 1 teaspoon salt
- ⅛ teaspoon clove
- 3 cups bread flour
- ⅛ teaspoon nutmeg
- 3 tablespoons sugar

- 1 grated orange zest
- ½ teaspoon cinnamon
- 1 ½ teaspoons active dry yeast
- 5 tablespoons butter/margarine

16 Slices/2 pounds
- 3 eggs
- 1 cup milk
- 1 ½ teaspoon salt
- ¼ teaspoon clove
- 4 cups bread flour
- ¼ teaspoon nutmeg
- 4 tablespoons sugar
- 1 ½ grated orange zest
- 1 ½ teaspoon cinnamon
- 2 teaspoons active dry yeast
- 6 tablespoons butter/margarine

Directions:
1. Place ingredients in the bread machine pan according to the manufacturer's recommended order.
2. Select the Light/Sweet Bread Cycle on your bread machine, and press Start.
3. When the bread is done, unplug the machine and remove the pan.
4. Let it rest for 5 minutes.
5. Gently remove the bread from the pan and place it on a cooling rack.
6. Slice after 10 minutes and enjoy!

Nutrition:
Per Serving Calories: 2300, Total Fat: 777g, Saturated Fat: 44g, Carbohydrates: 336g, Fiber: 12.6g, Sodium: 2966mg, Protein: 60.4g

Tip: You can substitute fresh orange zest for bottled zest or even use lemon zest in case of availability issues.

46. Toasted Walnut Bread

Prep Time: 10 minutes or less
Ready Time: 3 hours 10 minutes

12 Slices/1 ½ pounds
- 2 egg whites
- ¾ cup water
- 1 teaspoon salt
- 3 cups bread flour
- 1 ½ tablespoons white sugar
- 1 ½ tablespoons nonfat dry milk
- 1 ½ teaspoons bread machine yeast
- 2 tablespoons butter/margarine, cubed
- 1 cup walnuts, toasted & roughly-chopped

16 Slices/2 pounds
- 3 egg whites
- 1 cup water
- 1 ½ teaspoon salt
- 4 cups bread flour
- 2 tablespoons white sugar
- 2 tablespoons nonfat dry milk
- 2 teaspoons bread machine yeast
- 3 tablespoons butter/margarine, cubed
- 1 ½ cup walnuts, toasted & roughly-chopped

Directions:
1. Place ingredients in the bread machine pan according to the manufacturer's recommended order.
2. Select the Basic Bread Cycle with Medium crust on your bread machine, and press Start.
3. When the bread is done, unplug the machine and remove the pan.
4. Let it rest for 5 minutes.
5. Gently remove the bread from the pan and place it on a cooling rack.
6. Slice after 10 minutes and enjoy!

Nutrition:
Per Serving Calories: 187, Total Fat: 6.4g, Saturated Fat: 2g, Carbohydrates: 26.8g, Fiber: 1.5g, Sodium: 168mg, Protein: 6.1g

Tip: Add the walnuts with the flour in the beginning if you want them to mix in the bread completely for a subtle taste.

47. Chives & Sour Cream Bread

Prep Time: 10 minutes or less
Ready Time: 3 hours 10 minutes

12 Slices/1 ½ pounds
- 1 ½ teaspoons salt
- ¼ cup sour cream
- 3 cups bread flour
- 1 ½ tablespoons sugar
- ¼ cup minced chives
- ⅛ teaspoon baking soda
- 2 ¼ teaspoons active dry yeast
- ⅔ cup milk, room temperature
- 2 tablespoons butter/margarine
- ¼ cup water, room temperature

16 Slices/2 pounds
- 1 ½ teaspoons salt
- ¼ cup sour cream
- 4 cups bread flour
- 2 tablespoons sugar
- ⅓ cup minced chives
- ¼ teaspoon baking soda
- 2 ½ teaspoons active dry yeast
- ¾ cups milk, room temperature
- 3 tablespoons butter/margarine
- ⅓ cup water, room temperature

Directions:
1. Place ingredients in the bread machine pan according to the manufacturer's recommended order.
2. Select the Basic Bread Cycle with Crust color and loaf size on your bread machine, and press Start.
3. After 5 minutes of dough making, check it if needs extra water or flour.
4. When the bread is cooked, unplug the machine and remove the pan.
5. Let it rest for 5 minutes.
6. Gently remove the bread from the pan and place it on a cooling rack.
7. Slice after 10 minutes and enjoy!

Nutrition:
Per Serving Calories: 1850, Total Fat: 45g, Saturated Fat: 26g, Carbohydrates: 306g, Fiber: 12.3g, Sodium: 3932mg, Protein: 50g

Tip: Avoid making this recipe with the time delay feature.

48. Caramelized Onion & Yeast Bread

Prep Time: 30 minutes or less
Ready Time: 3 hours 30 minutes

12 Slices/1 ½ pounds
- 1 cup water
- 1 teaspoon salt
- 3 cups bread flour
- 2 tablespoon sugar
- 1 tablespoon butter
- 1 tablespoon olive oil
- 1 large onion, sliced
- 1 ½ teaspoons active dry yeast/ 1 teaspoon bread yeast

16 Slices/2 pounds
- 1 ¼ cups water
- 1 ½ teaspoon salt
- 4 cups bread flour
- 3 tablespoons sugar
- 2 tablespoon butter
- 2 tablespoon olive oil
- 2 medium onions, sliced
- 2 teaspoons active dry yeast/ 1 ½ teaspoons bread yeast

Directions:
1. Cook onions in butter in a skillet for 10 to 15 minutes over medium-low heat.
2. Stir frequently until the onions turn brown and then remove from heat.
3. Meanwhile, place ingredients except caramelized onions in the bread machine pan according to the manufacturer's recommended order.
4. Select the Basic Bread Cycle with Medium Crust color.

5. Once the machine signals 10 to 15 minutes before ending the kneading, add in your onions.
6. When the bread is cooked, unplug the machine and remove the pan.
7. Let it rest for 5 minutes.
8. Gently remove the bread from the pan and place it on a cooling rack.
9. Slice after 10 minutes and enjoy!

Nutrition:
Per Serving Calories: 140, Total Fat: 1.9g, Saturated Fat: 0.6g, Carbohydrates: 26g, Fiber: 1.2g, Sodium: 153mg, Protein: 3.5g

Tip: You can substitute 1 cup of bread flour with whole wheat flour or rye flour for better flavor or if you are short on bread flour.

49. Sunflower Seed Yeast Bread

Prep Time: 30 minutes or less
Ready Time: 3 hours 30 minutes

12 Slices/1 ½ pounds
- 1 ¼ cups water
- ½ teaspoon salt
- 2 tablespoons butter
- 3 tablespoons honey
- 2 tablespoons dry milk
- ½ cup sunflower seeds
- 2 ½ cups white bread flour
- ¾ cup wheat bread flour
- 3 teaspoons active dry yeast or 2 teaspoons fast rise yeast

16 Slices/2 pounds
- 2 cups water
- 1 teaspoon salt
- 3 tablespoons butter
- 4 tablespoons honey
- 3 tablespoons dry milk
- ⅔ cup sunflower seeds
- 3 cups white bread flour
- 1 cup wheat bread flour
- 4 teaspoons active dry yeast or 3 teaspoons fast rise yeast

Directions:
1. Place ingredients in the bread machine pan according to the manufacturer's recommended order.
2. Bake according to your manufacturer's recommended settings and time.
3. This recipe can easily be cooked with normal, quick or delayed time cycles.
4. When the bread is cooked, unplug the machine and remove the pan.
5. Let it rest for 5 minutes.
6. Gently remove the bread from the pan and place it on a cooling rack!
7. Slice after 10 minutes and enjoy!

Nutrition:
Per Serving Calories: 140, Total Fat: 1.9g, Saturated Fat: 0.6g, Carbohydrates: 26g, Fiber: 1.2g, Sodium: 153mg, Protein: 3.5g

Tip: Make sure all the ingredients are room temperature. Also, if you're using unsalted sunflower seeds, add a pinch more salt in the bread for enhanced flavor.

50. Cajun Herb Bread

Prep Time: 10 minutes or less
Ready Time: 2 hours 30 minutes

12 Slices/1 ½ pounds
- 1 cup water
- 3 cups bread flour
- ½ cup chopped onion
- 1 ½ teaspoons active dry yeast
- 1 ½ tablespoons granulated sugar
- ½ cup chopped green bell pepper
- 2 ½ teaspoons finely-chopped garlic
- 1 ½ teaspoon Cajun or Creole seasoning
- 2 ½ teaspoons unsalted butter, soft and cubed

16 Slices/2 pounds
- 1 ½ cups water
- 4 cups bread flour
- 1 cup chopped onion
- 2 teaspoons active dry yeast
- 2 tablespoons granulated sugar
- 1 cup chopped green bell pepper

- 3 teaspoons finely-chopped garlic
- 2 teaspoon Cajun or Creole seasoning
- 3 teaspoons unsalted butter, soft and cubed

Directions:

1. Place ingredients in the bread machine pan according to the manufacturer's recommended order.
2. Select the Basic/White Bread Cycle with Medium or Dark Crust on your bread machine, and press Start.
3. When the bread is done, unplug the machine and remove the pan.
4. Let it rest for 5 minutes.
5. Gently remove the bread from the pan and place it on a cooling rack.
6. Slice after 30 minutes and enjoy!

Nutrition:

Per Serving Calories: 47, Total Fat: 2g, Saturated Fat: 26g, Carbohydrates: 7g, Fiber: 1g, Sodium: 215mg, Protein: 1g

Tip: Avoid making this recipe with the time delay feature.

51. Roasted Garlic Clove Bread

Prep Time: 20 minutes or less
Ready Time: 1 hour 20 minutes

12 Slices/1 ½ pounds

- ½ cup milk
- 1 cup water
- 1 ½ teaspoon salt
- 3 ¾ cups bread flour
- 2 ½ tablespoons sugar
- 5 garlic cloves, minced
- 1 teaspoon garlic powder
- 3 ½ tablespoons unsalted butter
- 2 teaspoons bread machine yeast
- ½ cup grated Parmesan cheese
- 2 large head garlic, roasted for ⅓ cup mashed garlic

16 Slices/2 pounds

- 1 cup milk
- 1 ½ cups water

- 2 teaspoons salt
- 4 ¾ cups bread flour
- 3 tablespoons sugar
- 6 garlic cloves, minced
- 1 ½ teaspoons garlic powder
- 4 tablespoons unsalted butter
- 2 ½ teaspoons bread machine yeast
- 1 cup grated Parmesan cheese
- 2 large head garlic, roasted for ½ cup mashed garlic

Directions:

1. Squeeze garlic from the roasted garlic head to get the required ¼ cup quantity and set aside.
2. Mix butter and 6 minced garlic cloves in a microwave-safe bowl and microwave for 1-2 minutes until the garlic releases fragrance.
3. Place all the ingredients except roasted mashed garlic in the bread machine pan according to the manufacturer's recommended order.
4. Keep a check on the dough. If the kneading sounds rough, add more water. If the dough is sticky, add more flour.
5. Once the machine beeps for fruit/nut/mix-in ingredients, add in the roasted mashed garlic.
6. Select the Basic/White Bread cycle with Medium or Light Crust.
7. When the bread is done, unplug the machine and remove the pan.
8. Let it rest for 5 minutes.
9. Gently remove the bread from the pan and place it on a cooling rack.
10. Slice after 10 minutes and enjoy!

Nutrition:

Per Serving Calories: 203, Total Fat: 5g, Saturated Fat: 3g, Carbohydrates: 32g, Fiber: 1g, Sodium: 305mg, Protein: 6g

Tip: To roast a whole garlic head, first remove the loose papery skin of the garlic without removing all of it or loosening the cloves. Then turn the garlic on its side and cut the pointed head from the top until the raw cloves are visible. Place the garlic head with the raw cloves facing up on a square foil. Drizzle olive oil over the top and side of the garlic head and wrap the garlic in the foil. Preheat oven at 400 degrees and roast the foiled garlic on a baking pan in the oven for 40 minutes or until the cloves are golden-brown and soft. Remove the garlic from the oven, let it cool and gently separate the cloves and mash them to use!

52. Rosemary Italian Peasant Bread

Prep Time: 10 minutes or less
Ready Time: 2 hours 55 minutes

12 Slices/1 ½ pounds
- 1 cup water
- 1 ½ tablespoons yeast
- 2 ½ tablespoons olive oil
- 2 tablespoons sugar
- 3 cups all-purpose flour
- 1 ½ tablespoon salt plus extra salt
- 2 tablespoons rosemary plus extra rosemary

16 Slices/2 pounds
- 1 ½ cups water
- 2 tablespoons yeast
- 3 tablespoons olive oil
- 2 ½ tablespoons sugar
- 4 cups all-purpose flour
- 2 tablespoons salt plus extra salt
- 2 ½ tablespoons rosemary plus extra rosemary

Directions:
1. Place ingredients in the bread machine pan according to the manufacturer's recommended order.
2. Select the Basic/White Bread Cycle with Medium Crust on your bread machine, and press Start.
3. When the bread is done, unplug the machine and remove the pan.
4. Let it rest for 5 minutes.
5. Gently remove the bread from the pan and place it on a cooling rack.
6. Slice after 30 minutes and enjoy with extra salt and rosemary on top!

Nutrition:
Per Serving Calories: 632, Total Fat: 15.3g, Saturated Fat: 2.1g, Carbohydrates: 107.6g, Fiber: 5.2g, Sodium: 3497mg, Protein: 15.4g

Tip: You can decrease the amount of salt by half if you fear the yeast may not rise or if you prefer a less salty flavor.

Chapter 7: Cheese Bread Recipes

53. Cream Cheese Yeast Bread

Prep Time: 10 minutes or less
Ready Time: 50 minutes

12 Slices/1 ½ pounds
- ½ cup water
- 1 beaten egg
- ¾ teaspoon salt
- 3 cups bread flour
- 3 tablespoons sugar
- 1 ⅔ tablespoons butter, melted
- ½ cup cream cheese, softened
- 1 ½ teaspoons active dry yeast

16 Slices/2 pounds
- 1 cup water
- 2 beaten eggs
- 1 teaspoon salt
- 4 cups bread flour
- 4 tablespoons sugar
- 3 tablespoons butter, melted
- 1 cup cream cheese, softened
- 2 ½ teaspoons active dry yeast

Directions:
1. Place ingredients in the bread machine pan according to the manufacturer's recommended order.
2. Process the ingredients in a dough cycle and take out the dough on a flat surface.
3. Form the dough into a loaf and place in a greased 9x5 loaf pan.
4. Cover the loaf with a clean cloth and let it rise until it doubles in size.
5. Bake the loaf for 35 minutes in an oven at 350 degrees.
6. Take out the loaf and let it rest on a cooling rack.
7. Slice after 10 minutes and enjoy!

Nutrition:
Per Serving Calories: 1500, Total Fat: 47g, Saturated Fat: 26g, Carbohydrates: 229g, Fiber: 7g, Sodium: 1990mg, Protein: 36g

Tip: You can substitute butter with oil in case of availability issues and can add extra water in the dough if it's too stiff. Make sure to start with room temperature ingredients.

54. Sharp Cheese Yeast Bread

Prep Time: 10 minutes or less
Ready Time: 3 hours 10 minutes

12 Slices/1 ½ pounds
- 1 ¼ cups water
- 1 teaspoon salt
- 3 cups bread flour
- 2 tablespoons sugar
- 1 tablespoon soft butter
- ⅓ cup Parmesan cheese
- ¼ cup nonfat dry milk powder
- 1 teaspoon coarse black pepper
- 1 ½ cups grated sharp cheddar cheese, room temperature
- 2 ¼ teaspoon active dry yeast or 1 ½ teaspoon instant yeast

16 Slices/2 pounds
- 1 ½ cups water
- 1 ½ teaspoon salt
- 4 cups bread flour
- 3 tablespoons sugar
- 2 tablespoons soft butter
- ½ cup Parmesan cheese
- ⅓ cup nonfat dry milk powder
- 2 teaspoons coarse black pepper
- 2 cups grated sharp cheddar cheese, room temperature
- 2 ½ teaspoons active dry yeast or 2 teaspoons instant yeast

Directions:
1. Place ingredients in the bread machine pan according to the manufacturer's recommended order.
2. The wet ingredients are usually added first to the bottom of the pan, followed with the dry ingredients to cover the wet ingredients.

3. Select the Basic Bread Cycle/White on your bread machine, and press Start.
4. When the bread is done, unplug the machine and remove the pan.
5. Let it rest for 5 minutes.
6. Gently remove the bread from the pan, and place it on a cooling rack.
7. Slice after 10 minutes and enjoy!

Nutrition:
Per Serving Calories: 2528, Total Fat: 81g, Saturated Fat: 49g, Carbohydrates: 334g, Fiber: 12g, Sodium: 4169mg, Protein: 107g

Tip: You can substitute dry milk with liquid milk, or omit it altogether if you are short on any of them.

55. Feta Cheese Yeast Bread

Prep Time: 10 minutes or less
Ready Time: 3 hours 10 minutes

12 Slices/1 ½ pounds
- 1 teaspoon salt
- 3 cups bread flour
- 2 teaspoons olive oil
- 1 cup buttermilk, warm
- 1 tablespoon white sugar
- ⅓ cup crumbled feta cheese
- 2 teaspoons bread machine yeast
- ½ cup black olives, halved and pitted

16 Slices/2 pounds
- 1 ½ teaspoons salt
- 4 cups bread flour
- 3 teaspoons olive oil
- 1 ½ cups buttermilk, warm
- 2 tablespoons white sugar
- ½ cup crumbled feta cheese
- 2 ½ teaspoons bread machine yeast
- 1 cup black olives, halved and pitted

Directions:
1. Assemble the ingredients and place them in the pan except for the olives according to the manufacturer's recommended order.
2. Select the Basic Bread Cycle on your machine, and Start.

3. Once the machine beeps for mix-in ingredients, add in the olives.
4. Once the loaf is done, remove the pan and let it cool on a cooling rack.
5. Slice after 10 minutes and enjoy!

Nutrition:
Per Serving Calories: 152, Total Fat: 2g, Saturated Fat: 1g, Carbohydrates: 26g, Fiber: 1g, Sodium: 312mg, Protein: 4g

Tip: Make sure the ingredients are at room temperature.

56. Jalapeno & Cheese Bread

Prep Time: 30 minutes or less
Ready Time: 2 hours 30 minutes

12 Slices/1 ½ pounds
- 2 eggs
- ¼ cup water
- 1 ½ teaspoon salt
- ¾ cup sour cream
- 2 tablespoons sugar
- 3 cups all-purpose flour
- ¼ teaspoon baking soda
- 2 teaspoons active dry yeast
- 1 cup grated sharp cheddar cheese
- 3 tablespoons fresh jalapeno peppers, seeded and chopped

16 Slices/2 pounds
- 3 eggs
- ⅓ cup water
- 2 teaspoons salt
- 1 cup sour cream
- 3 tablespoons sugar
- 4 cups all-purpose flour
- ⅓ teaspoon baking soda
- 3 teaspoons active dry yeast
- 1 ½ cup grated sharp cheddar cheese
- 4 tablespoons fresh jalapeno peppers, seeded and chopped

Directions:

1. Assemble the ingredients and place them in the pan according to the manufacturer's recommended order.
2. Select the Light Crust Bread Cycle on your machine, and Start.
3. Once the machine beeps for mix-in ingredients, add in the olives.
4. Once the loaf is done, remove the pan and let it cool on a cooling rack.
5. Slice after an hour and enjoy!

Nutrition:
Per Serving Calories: 273, Total Fat: 9g, Saturated Fat: 5g, Carbohydrates: 36g, Fiber: 1g, Sodium: 556mg, Protein: 9g

Tip: You can substitute fresh jalapenos with the canned version in case of availability issues. Make sure to dice it before adding to the recipe.

57. Ricotta Cheese & Yeast Bread

Prep Time: 10 minutes or less
Ready Time: 3 hours

12 Slices/1 ½ pounds
- ⅓ cup milk
- 1 beaten egg
- 1 teaspoon salt
- 3 cups bread flour
- ¼ cup white sugar
- 15 ounces ricotta cheese
- 2 ½ teaspoons active dry yeast
- 2 tablespoons melted butter, cooled

16 Slices/2 pounds
- ½ cup milk
- 2 beaten eggs
- 1 ½ teaspoons salt
- 4 cups bread flour
- ⅓ cup white sugar
- 550 grams ricotta cheese
- 3 teaspoons active dry yeast
- 3 tablespoons melted butter, cooled

Directions:
1. Assemble the ingredients and place them in the pan according to the manufacturer's recommended order.

2. Select the Basic Bread Cycle on your machine, and Start.
3. Once the loaf is done, remove the pan and let it cool on a cooling rack.
4. Slice after 10 minutes and enjoy!

Nutrition:
Per Serving Calories: 206, Total Fat: 5g, Saturated Fat: 1g, Carbohydrates: 30g, Fiber: 1g, Sodium: 132mg, Protein: 8g

Tip: Make sure the ingredients are at room temperature.

58. Pepperoni & Cheese Bread

Prep Time: 10 minutes or less
Ready Time: 10 minutes

12 Slices/1 ½ pounds
- 2 tablespoons sugar
- 3 ¼ cups bread flour
- 1 ½ teaspoons oregano
- ⅔ cup diced pepperoni
- 1 ½ teaspoons garlic salt
- 1 ½ teaspoons active dry yeast
- ⅓ cup shredded mozzarella cheese
- 1 cup plus 2 tablespoons warm water

16 Slices/2 pounds
- 3 tablespoons sugar
- 4 cups bread flour
- 2 teaspoons oregano
- 2 teaspoons garlic salt
- 1 ½ cups warm water
- ¾ cup diced pepperoni
- 2 teaspoons active dry yeast
- ½ cup shredded mozzarella cheese

Directions:
1. Assemble the ingredients and place them in the pan according to the manufacturer's recommended order
2. Or start with wet ingredients first, and dry afterwards except pepperoni.
3. Select the Basic Bread Cycle with Medium Crust on your machine, and Start.
4. Once the machine beeps in the final stages of kneading, add in the pepperoni.

5. Once the loaf is done, remove the pan and let it cool on a cooling rack.
6. Slice after 10 minutes and enjoy!

Nutrition:
Per Serving Calories: 1710, Total Fat: 12g, Saturated Fat: 5g, Carbohydrates: 339g, Fiber: 12g, Sodium: 250mg, Protein: 52g

Tip: We do not recommend using the delay time feature with this recipe.

59. Cottage Cheese & Dill Bread

Prep Time: 5 minutes or less
Ready Time: 2 hours 5 minutes

12 Slices/1 ½ pounds
- 1 teaspoon salt
- 1 ½ teaspoon yeast
- 1 cup hot water
- 3 cups bread flour
- 3 teaspoons sugar
- 2 tablespoons butter
- 3 teaspoons dry milk
- 3 teaspoons dill weed
- ⅔ cup cottage cheese
- 3 teaspoons instant minced onion

16 Slices/2 pounds
- 1 ½ teaspoons salt
- 2 teaspoons yeast
- 1 ½ cups hot water
- 4 cups bread flour
- 4 teaspoons sugar
- 3 tablespoons butter
- 4 teaspoons dry milk
- 4 teaspoons dill weed
- ¾ cup cottage cheese
- 4 teaspoons instant minced onion

Directions:
1. Assemble the ingredients and place them in the pan according to the manufacturer's recommended order.
2. Select the Basic Bread Cycle with Light Crust on your machine, and Start.

3. Once the loaf is done, remove the pan and let it cool on a cooling rack.
4. Slice after 10 minutes and enjoy!

Nutrition:
Per Serving Calories: 99, Total Fat: 1g, Saturated Fat: 0g, Carbohydrates: 17g, Fiber: 0g, Sodium: 188mg, Protein: 3g

Tip: You can make this recipe with the quick bread setting as well. Plus, you can substitute cottage cheese with yogurt if you're short on cheese.

60. Simple Oregano & Cheese Bread

Prep Time: 10 minutes or less
Ready Time: 2 hours 10 minutes

12 Slices/1 ½ pounds
- 1 cup water
- 1 teaspoon salt
- 3 cups bread flour
- 3 tablespoons sugar
- 1 ½ tablespoons olive oil
- ½ cup freshly grated cheese
- 2 teaspoons active dry yeast
- 1 tablespoon dried leaf oregano

16 Slices/2 pounds
- 1 ½ water
- 1 ½ teaspoons salt
- 4 cups bread flour
- 4 tablespoons sugar
- 2 tablespoons olive oil
- 1 cup freshly grated cheese
- 3 teaspoons active dry yeast
- 1 ½ tablespoons dried leaf oregano

Directions:
1. Assemble the ingredients and place them in the pan according to the manufacturer's recommended order.
2. Select the Basic Bread Cycle with Medium Crust on your machine, and Start.
3. Once the loaf is done, remove the pan and let it cool on a cooling rack.
4. Slice after 10 minutes and enjoy!

Nutrition:
Per Serving Calories: 61, Total Fat: 3g, Saturated Fat: 1g, Carbohydrates: 7g, Fiber: 1g, Sodium: 188mg, Protein: 2g

Tip: If you like, you can simply prepare the dough in the bread machine by using the dough cycle. And then, take the dough out to make a free-form loaf in the oven at 400 degrees for 35 minutes for personal preference.

61. Cheese & Scallion Bread

Prep Time: 10 minutes or less
Ready Time: 3 hours

12 Slices/1 ½ pounds
- ½ cup milk
- ⅛ cup water
- 2 beaten egg
- ½ teaspoon salt
- 3 cups bread flour
- 1 ⅛ teaspoons white sugar
- 2 tablespoons butter, softened
- 1 ⅛ teaspoons active dry yeast
- 2 tablespoons green scallions, finely-chopped
- 1 ½ cups shredded extra-sharp cheddar cheese

16 Slices/2 pounds
- ⅔ cup milk
- ¼ cup water
- 3 beaten egg
- 1 teaspoon salt
- 4 cups bread flour
- 1 ¼ teaspoons white sugar
- 3 tablespoons butter, softened
- 1 ¼ teaspoons active dry yeast
- 3 tablespoons green scallions, finely-chopped
- 1 ⅔ cups shredded extra-sharp cheddar cheese

Directions:
1. Assemble the ingredients and place them in the pan according to the manufacturer's recommended order.

2. Select the Basic Bread Cycle on your machine, and Start.
3. Once the loaf is done, remove the pan and let it cool on a cooling rack.
4. Slice after 10 minutes and enjoy!

Nutrition:
Per Serving Calories: 192, Total Fat: 6g, Saturated Fat: 1g, Carbohydrates: 25g, Fiber: 0g, Sodium: 245mg, Protein: 7g

Tip: Make sure the ingredients are at room temperature.

62. Easy Cottage Cheese Bread

Prep Time: 5 minutes or less
Ready Time: 3 hours 5 minutes

12 Slices/1 ½ pounds
- 1 egg
- ½ cup water
- 1 teaspoon salt
- 3 cups bread flour
- 1 cup cottage cheese
- 1 tablespoon white sugar
- ¼ teaspoon baking soda
- 2 tablespoons margarine
- 2 ½ teaspoons active dry yeast

16 Slices/2 pounds
- 2 eggs
- 1 cup water
- 1 ½ teaspoons salt
- 4 cups bread flour
- 1 ½ cup cottage cheese
- 2 tablespoons white sugar
- ⅓ teaspoon baking soda
- 3 tablespoons margarine
- 3 teaspoons active dry yeast

Directions:
1. Assemble the ingredients and place them in the pan according to the manufacturer's recommended order.
2. Select the Basic Bread/Light Cycle on your machine, and Start.

3. Once the loaf is done, remove the pan and let it cool on a cooling rack.
4. Slice after 10 minutes and enjoy!

Nutrition:
Per Serving Calories: 171, Total Fat: 4g, Saturated Fat: 1g, Carbohydrates: 27g, Fiber: 1g, Sodium: 324mg, Protein: 7g
Tip: You can add ½ cup more flour to adjust the dough if it is too sticky.

63. Cheese Bread with Pepperoni

Prep Time: 10 minutes or less
Ready Time: 4 hours 5 minutes

12 Slices/1 ½ pounds
- ½ teaspoon salt
- 3 cups bread flour
- 1 cup warm water
- 1 tablespoon butter
- 2 tablespoons sugar
- ¼ teaspoon garlic powder
- 1 cup chopped pepperoni
- 2 teaspoons ground mustard
- ½ teaspoon cayenne pepper
- 2 ¼ teaspoons active dry yeast
- 1 ½ cups shredded Mexican cheese blend

16 Slices/2 pounds
- 1 teaspoon salt
- 4 cups bread flour
- 1 ½ cup warm water
- 1 ½ tablespoon butter
- 2 ½ tablespoons sugar
- ½ teaspoon garlic powder
- 1 ½ cup chopped pepperoni
- 2 ½ teaspoons ground mustard
- 1 teaspoon cayenne pepper
- 2 ½ teaspoons active dry yeast
- 1 ¾ cups shredded Mexican cheese blend

Directions:
1. Assemble the ingredients and place them in the pan according to the manufacturer's recommended order
2. Or start with wet ingredients first, and dry afterwards except cheese and pepperoni.

3. Select the Basic Bread Cycle with Crust and loaf size of your choice, and Start.
4. Once the machine beeps in the final stages of kneading, add in the cheese and pepperoni.
5. Once the loaf is done, remove the pan and let it cool on a cooling rack.
6. Slice after 10 minutes and enjoy!

Nutrition:
Per Serving Calories: 177, Total Fat: 8g, Saturated Fat: 4g, Carbohydrates: 19g, Fiber: 1g, Sodium: 329mg, Protein: 7g

Tip: You can increase the amount of cheese and pepperoni if you would like a more enhanced flavor.

64. Cheese Bread with Jalapeno

Prep Time: 15 minutes or less
Ready Time: 2 hours 15 minutes

12 Slices/1 ½ pounds
- 1 cup water
- 3 cups bread flour
- 1 ½ teaspoons salt
- 1 ½ tablespoons sugar
- 1 small jalapeno pepper
- 2 teaspoons active dry yeast
- 3 tablespoons nonfat dry milk
- 1 ½ tablespoons unsalted butter, cubed
- ¼ cup finely shredded Mexican blend/Monterey Jack cheese

16 Slices/2 pounds
- 1 ½ cups water
- 4 cups bread flour
- 2 teaspoons salt
- 2 tablespoons sugar
- 2 small jalapeno pepper
- 2 ½ teaspoons active dry yeast
- 3 ½ tablespoons nonfat dry milk
- 2 tablespoons unsalted butter, cubed
- ⅓ cup finely shredded Mexican blend/Monterey Jack cheese

Directions:

1. Cut the stem of the pepper and slice lengthwise in half. Remove the seeds and finely chop the pepper.
2. Place all the ingredients in the bread machine pan according to the manufacturer's recommended order
3. Select the Basic Bread Cycle with Light or Medium Crust, and Start.
4. Once the loaf is done, remove the pan and let it cool on a cooling rack.
5. Slice after 10 minutes and enjoy!

Nutrition:
Per Serving Calories: 158, Total Fat: 3g, Saturated Fat: 1g, Carbohydrates: 27g, Fiber: 1g, Sodium: 298mg, Protein: 5g

Tip: You can substitute fresh pepper with canned pepper in case of an availability issue. Though stick to the original quantity.

65. Bacon & Cheddar Cheese Bread

Prep Time: 20 minutes or less
Ready Time: 2 hours 50 minutes

12 Slices/1 ½ pounds
- 1 cup water
- 1 ⅛ teaspoons salt
- 3 cups bread flour
- 1 ½ tablespoons vegetable oil
- 1 ½ teaspoons active dry yeast
- 2 tablespoons white sugar
- 1 ½ cups shredded Swiss cheese
- 2 ½ tablespoons nonfat dry milk
- 7 slices cooked bacon, crumbled

16 Slices/2 pounds
- 1 ⅓ cups water
- 1 ¼ teaspoons salt
- 4 cups bread flour
- 2 tablespoons vegetable oil
- 2 teaspoons active dry yeast
- 2 ½ tablespoons white sugar
- 2 cups shredded Swiss cheese
- 3 tablespoons nonfat dry milk
- 8 slices cooked bacon, crumbled

Directions:
1. Assemble the ingredients except cheese and bacon and place them in the pan according to the manufacturer's recommended order.
2. Select the Basic Bread Cycle with Crust and Loaf size of your choice, and Start.
3. Once the machine beeps in the final stages of kneading, add in the cheese and bacon.
4. Once the loaf is done, remove the pan and let it cool on a cooling rack.
5. Slice after 10 minutes and enjoy!

Nutrition:
Per Serving Calories: 357, Total Fat: 13g, Saturated Fat: 6g, Carbohydrates: 42g, Fiber: 2g, Sodium: 474mg, Protein: 17g

Tip: You can use either real bacon or imitation bits which you can find in the salad/dressing aisle at the grocery mart. Add 1/2 cup of real bacon or 1/4 cup of imitation bacon bits.

Chapter 8: Quick Bread Recipes

66. Pumpkin Spice Quick Bread

Prep Time: 10 minutes or less
Ready Time: 3 hours 10 minutes

12 Slices/1 ½ pounds
- 2 eggs
- 1 ½ cups sugar
- ½ teaspoon salt
- 1 ½ teaspoons vanilla
- ½ cup vegetable oil
- 1 cup chopped nuts
- 2 ½ cups all-purpose flour
- 1 ½ cups canned pumpkin
- ¼ teaspoon ground cloves
- 2 ½ teaspoons baking powder
- ½ teaspoon ground nutmeg
- 1 ½ teaspoons ground cinnamon

16 Slices/2 pounds
- 3 eggs
- 2 cups sugar
- 1 teaspoon salt
- 2 teaspoons vanilla
- 1 cup vegetable oil
- 1 ½ cup chopped nuts
- 3 ½ cups all-purpose flour
- 1 ⅔ cups canned pumpkin
- ½ teaspoon ground cloves

- 3 teaspoons baking powder
- 1 teaspoon ground nutmeg
- 2 teaspoons ground cinnamon

Directions:
1. Place ingredients in the bread machine pan according to the manufacturer's recommended order.
2. Select the Quick Bread Cycle on your bread machine, and press Start.
3. When the bread is done, unplug the machine and remove the pan.
4. Gently shake the bucket to remove the bread, and place it on a cooling rack.
5. Slice after 10 minutes and enjoy!

Nutrition:
Per Serving Calories: 200, Total Fat: 7g, Saturated Fat: 1g, Carbohydrates: 31g, Fiber: 1g, Sodium: 140mg, Protein: 3g

Tip: You can substitute all-purpose flour with bread flour if you are low on all-purpose flour.

67. Cranberry Quick Bread Loaf

Prep Time: 10 minutes or less
Ready Time: 1 hours 50 minutes

12 Slices/1 ½ pounds
- 2 eggs
- ¾ cup honey
- 1 teaspoon salt
- ⅓ cup warm milk
- 3 cups bread flour
- 1 teaspoon cinnamon
- 1 ½ teaspoon baking soda
- 1 cup chopped walnuts
- 2 ½ teaspoons vanilla extract
- 1 teaspoon baking powder
- 1 cup orange juice, warmed
- ⅓ cup cranberry juice, warmed
- 2 cups fresh or dried cranberries

16 Slices/2 pounds
- 3 eggs
- 1 cup honey
- 1 ½ teaspoons salt
- ½ cup warm milk
- 4 cups bread flour
- 1 ½ teaspoons cinnamon
- 2 teaspoons baking soda
- 1 ½ cup chopped walnuts
- 3 teaspoons vanilla extract
- 1 ½ teaspoon baking powder
- 1 ½ cup orange juice, warmed
- ½ cup cranberry juice, warmed
- 2 ½ cups fresh or dried cranberries

Directions:

1. Place ingredients in the bread machine pan according to the manufacturer's recommended order.
2. Select the Quick Bread Cycle with your choice of Crust and loaf size on your bread machine, and press Start.
3. When the bread is done, unplug the machine and remove the pan.
4. Gently shake the bucket to remove the bread, and place it on a cooling rack.
5. Slice after 10 minutes and enjoy!

Nutrition:

Per Serving Calories: 240, Total Fat: 5g, Saturated Fat: 1g, Carbohydrates: 44g, Fiber: 2g, Sodium: 333mg, Protein: 5g

Tip: You can store the bread in a freezer safe bag for up to 6 months. Or keep fresh in a cloth bread bag or bread box for 3 days.

68. Zucchini Quick Bread Loaf

Prep Time: 5 minutes or less
Ready Time: 1 hours 43 minutes

12 Slices/1 ½ pounds
- 2 eggs
- 1 cup honey
- 2 ½ cups flour
- 1 teaspoon salt
- 1 ½ teaspoons cinnamon
- 1 ½ cups shredded zucchini
- 1 teaspoon baking soda
- 1 teaspoon baking powder
- ⅓ cup unsweetened applesauce

16 Slices/2 pounds
- 3 eggs
- 1 ½ cups honey
- 3 ½ cups flour
- 1 ½ teaspoons salt
- 2 teaspoons cinnamon
- 2 cups shredded zucchini
- 1 ½ teaspoons baking soda
- 1 ½ teaspoons baking powder
- ½ cup unsweetened applesauce

Directions:

1. Place ingredients in the bread machine pan according to the manufacturer's recommended order.
2. Select the Quick Bread Cycle with your choice of Crust and loaf size on your bread machine, and press Start.
3. When the bread is done, unplug the machine and remove the pan.
4. Gently shake the bucket to remove the bread, and place it on a cooling rack.
5. Slice after 10 minutes and enjoy!

Nutrition:

Per Serving Calories: 138, Total Fat: 1g, Saturated Fat: 1g, Carbohydrates: 30g, Fiber: 1g, Sodium: 265mg, Protein: 3g

Tip: You can add chopped walnuts in the mix for an enhanced flavor.

69. Quick Banana Bread Loaf

Prep Time: 5 minutes or less
Ready Time: 1 hours 45 minutes

12 Slices/1 ½ pounds
- 2 eggs
- 1 teaspoon salt
- ¾ cup white sugar
- 1 teaspoon cinnamon
- 3 cups all-purpose flour
- ⅓ cup warm buttermilk
- 1 ½ teaspoons vanilla extract
- 1 ¼ teaspoons baking soda
- 1 teaspoon baking powder
- 3 medium-sized ripe bananas, mashed
- 1 cup butter, room temperature and cubed

16 Slices/2 pounds
- 3 eggs
- 1 ½ teaspoons salt
- 1 cup white sugar
- 1 ½ teaspoons cinnamon
- 4 cups all-purpose flour
- ½ cup warm buttermilk
- 2 teaspoons vanilla extract
- 1 ½ teaspoons baking soda

- 1 ½ teaspoons baking powder
- 4 medium-sized ripe bananas, mashed
- 1 ½ cups butter, room temperature and cubed

Directions:

1. Place ingredients in the bread machine pan according to the manufacturer's recommended order.
2. Select the Quick Bread Cycle with your choice of Crust and loaf size on your bread machine, and press Start.
3. When the bread is done, unplug the machine and remove the pan.
4. Gently shake the bucket to remove the bread, and place it on a cooling rack.
5. Slice after 10 minutes and enjoy!

Nutrition:

Per Serving) Calories: 316, Total Fat: 17g, Saturated Fat: 7g, Carbohydrates: 39g, Fiber: 2g, Sodium: 363mg, Protein: 5g

Tip: You can add chopped walnuts and chocolate chips during the mix-in beep to enhance the bread's flavor. Also, if your machine doesn't have a quick bread cycle, consult the manual for equivalent settings.

70. Classic White Bread with No Yeast

Prep Time: 5 minutes or less
Ready Time: 1 hours 45 minutes

12 Slices/1 ½ pounds

- 2 eggs
- ½ cup sugar
- 1 ½ cups milk
- 1 teaspoon butter
- ½ teaspoon salt
- 3 cups all-purpose flour
- 2 teaspoons baking powder
- 1 ½ tablespoons white vinegar or apple cider vinegar

16 Slices/2 pounds

- 3 eggs
- 1 cup sugar
- 2 cups milk

- 1 ½ teaspoons butter
- 1 teaspoon salt
- 4 cups all-purpose flour
- 2 ½ teaspoons baking powder
- 2 tablespoons white vinegar or apple cider vinegar

Directions:

1. Place ingredients in the bread machine pan according to the manufacturer's recommended order.
2. Select the Cake Bread Cycle (if available) or simply White Bread Cycle with your choice of Crust and loaf size on your bread machine, and press Start.
3. When the bread is done, unplug the machine and remove the pan.
4. Gently shake the bucket to remove the bread, and place it on a cooling rack.
5. Slice after 10 minutes and enjoy!

Nutrition:

Per Serving Calories: 175, Total Fat: 2g, Saturated Fat: 0.9g, Carbohydrates: 34.2g, Fiber: 0.9g, Sodium: 125mg, Protein: 5.2g

Tip: This bread won't rise much during the rise cycle but will do so during baking. If you have a custom setting on your bread machine, we would suggest mixing, kneading, and then baking the bread, so you won't need to use the rise cycle.

71. Cornmeal Quick Bread

Prep Time: 5 minutes or less
Ready Time: 45 minutes

12 Slices/1 ½ pounds

- 1 cup milk
- 1 teaspoon salt
- ⅞ cup cornmeal
- 2 ½ tablespoons sugar
- ⅓ cup melted butter
- 3 cups all-purpose flour
- 2 large eggs, lightly beaten
- 3 ½ teaspoons baking powder

16 Slices/2 pounds

- 1 ½ cups milk

- 1 ½ teaspoons salt
- 1 cup cornmeal
- 3 tablespoons sugar
- ½ cup melted butter
- 4 cups all-purpose flour
- 3 large eggs, lightly beaten
- 4 teaspoons baking powder

Directions:
1. Place ingredients in the bread machine pan according to the manufacturer's recommended order.
2. Select the Cake Bread Cycle (if available) or simply Regular Bread Cycle with your choice of crust and loaf size on your bread machine, and press Start.
3. When the bread is done, unplug the machine and remove the pan.
4. Gently shake the bucket to remove the bread, and place it on a cooling rack.
5. Slice after 10 minutes and enjoy!

Nutrition:
Per Serving Calories: 166, Total Fat: 2.5g, Saturated Fat: 4.1g, Carbohydrates: 21.7g, Fiber: 1.2g, Sodium: 212mg, Protein: 3.8g

Tip: You can substitute butter with vegetable oil and all-purpose flour with bread flour in case of availability issues.

72. No Yeast Quick Flatbread

Prep Time: 5 minutes or less
Ready Time: 30 minutes

12 Slices/1 ½ pounds
- 1 ½ cups whole milk
- 3 cups plain flour
- 1 ½ tablespoons olive oil
- A few pinches salt & pepper
- 1 ½ tablespoons garlic puree
- 2 ½ tablespoons melted butter

16 Slices/2 pounds
- 2 cups whole milk
- 4 cups plain flour
- 2 tablespoons olive oil

- A few pinches salt & pepper
- 2 tablespoons garlic puree
- 3 tablespoons melted butter

Directions:
1. Place ingredients in the bread machine pan according to the manufacturer's recommended order.
2. Select the Regular Bread Cycle with your choice of crust and loaf size on your bread machine, and press Start.
3. When the flatbread is done, unplug the machine and remove the pan.
4. Gently shake the bucket to remove the bread, and place it on a cooling rack.
5. Serve and enjoy with chicken!

Nutrition:
Per Serving Calories: 474, Total Fat: 11g, Saturated Fat: 6g, Carbohydrates: 79g, Fiber: 3g, Sodium: 80mg, Protein: 12g

Tip: You can substitute plain flour with all-purpose flour in case of availability issues.

73. No Yeast Tutti Frutti Bread Cake

Prep Time: 5 minutes or less
Ready Time: 1 hour 55 minutes

12 Slices/1 ½ pounds
- ½ cup oil
- 1 pinch salt
- 1 cup warm milk
- 1 teaspoon vinegar
- 1 cup candied fruit
- 4 tablespoons sugar
- 1 teaspoon baking soda
- 3 cups all-purpose flour
- 1 teaspoon vanilla extract
- 1 teaspoon baking powder
- 1 ¾ cups sweetened condensed milk

16 Slices/2 pounds
- 1 cup oil
- A few pinches salt
- 1 ½ cups warm milk
- 1 ½ teaspoons vinegar

- 1 ½ cups candied fruit
- 4 ½ tablespoons sugar
- 1 ½ teaspoon baking soda
- 4 cups all-purpose flour
- 1 ½ teaspoons vanilla extract
- 1 ½ teaspoon baking powder
- 1 ⅞ cups sweetened condensed milk

Directions:
1. Place ingredients except tutti frutti in the bread machine pan according to the manufacturer's recommended order.
2. Add the tutti frutti during the finishing stages of the kneading cycle.
3. Select the Quick Bread or Cake Bread cycle with your choice of crust and loaf size on your bread machine, and press Start.
4. When the cake bread is done, unplug the machine and remove the pan.
5. Gently shake the bucket to remove the cake bread, and place it on a cooling rack.
6. Slice after 25 minutes and enjoy!

Nutrition:
Per Serving Calories: 327, Total Fat: 13g, Saturated Fat: 3g, Carbohydrates: 46g, Fiber: 1g, Sodium: 178mg, Protein: 6g

Tip: You can substitute white sugar with organic cane sugar or even brown sugar for a healthier approach and enhanced flavor.

74. Pumpkin Pie Spice Quick Bread

Prep Time: 5 minutes or less
Ready Time: 1 hour 45 minutes

12 Slices/1 ½ pounds
- 2 eggs
- ½ teaspoon salt
- ½ cup canola oil
- 1 ½ teaspoons vanilla
- 1 cup brown sugar
- 1 cup white sugar
- 1 ½ cups canned pumpkin
- 3 cups all-purpose flour
- 1 cup chopped walnuts
- 2 ¼ teaspoons baking powder

- 2 teaspoons pumpkin pie spice

16 Slices/2 pounds
- 3 eggs
- 1 teaspoon salt
- 1 cup canola oil
- 2 teaspoons vanilla
- 1 ½ cup brown sugar
- 1 ½ cup white sugar
- 2 cups canned pumpkin
- 4 cups all-purpose flour
- 1 ½ cups chopped walnuts
- 2 ½ teaspoons baking powder
- 2 ½ teaspoons pumpkin pie spice

Directions:
1. Place ingredients in the bread machine pan according to the manufacturer's recommended order.
2. Add chopped walnuts during the finishing stages of the kneading cycle when the machine beeps for mix-in ingredients.
3. Select the Quick Bread or Cake Bread cycle with Medium Crust and loaf size on your bread machine, and press Start.
4. When the bread is done, unplug the machine and remove the pan.
5. Gently shake the bucket to remove the cake bread, and place it on a cooling rack.
6. Slice after 25 minutes and enjoy!

Nutrition:
Per Serving Calories: 225, Total Fat: 10g, Saturated Fat: 1g, Carbohydrates: 31g, Fiber: 1g, Sodium: 31mg, Protein: 4g

Tip: Serve this delicious bread with creamy butter to get the full experience.

75. Jalapeno Cheese Quick Cornbread

Prep Time: 5 minutes or less
Ready Time: 1 hour 50 minutes

12 Slices/1 ½ pounds
- 1 cup milk
- 1 teaspoon salt
- 2 eggs, lightly beaten
- 1 cup all-purpose flour
- 1 ½ cups yellow cornmeal
- 3 teaspoons baking powder
- 8 tablespoons unsalted butter
- ¼ cup jalapenos, finely-chopped
- 1 ½ cups shredded cheddar cheese
- 2 tablespoons granulated white sugar

16 Slices/2 pounds
- 1 ½ cups milk
- 1 ½ teaspoons salt
- 2 eggs, lightly beaten
- 1 ½ cups all-purpose flour
- 2 cups yellow cornmeal
- 3 ½ teaspoons baking powder
- 8 ½ tablespoons unsalted butter
- ⅓ cup jalapenos, finely-chopped
- 1 cup shredded cheddar cheese
- 2 ½ tablespoons granulated white sugar

Directions:
1. Place ingredients in the bread machine pan according to the manufacturer's recommended order.
2. Select the Quick Bread cycle with Light Crust and loaf size on your bread machine, and press Start.
3. When the bread is done, unplug the machine and remove the pan.
4. Gently shake the bucket to remove the cake bread, and place it on a cooling rack.
5. Slice after 25 minutes and enjoy!

Nutrition:
Per Serving Calories: 270, Total Fat: 10g, Saturated Fat: 9g, Carbohydrates: 26g, Fiber: 12g, Sodium: 409mg, Protein: 8g

Tip: We recommend you to use the type of jalapenos that fit your heat level. If you don't like them, simply decrease their amount or omit them altogether.

76. Yeast Free Quick Chocolate Cake

Prep Time: 10 minutes or less
Ready Time: 1 hour 40 minutes

12 Slices/1 ½ pounds
- 2 eggs
- 1 ½ cup milk
- 1 ½ teaspoons salt
- 3 cups all-purpose flour
- 1 ½ teaspoons baking soda
- 2 ½ teaspoons vanilla extract
- 1 ½ teaspoons baking powder
- 2 cups light brown sugar
- 12 ½ tablespoons unsalted butter
- 1 cup unsweetened cocoa powder
- ⅞ cup mini semi-sweet chocolate chips

16 Slices/2 pounds
- 3 eggs
- 2 cups milk
- 2 teaspoons salt
- 4 cups all-purpose flour
- 2 teaspoons baking soda
- 3 teaspoons vanilla extract
- 2 teaspoons baking powder
- 2 ½ cups light brown sugar
- 13 tablespoons unsalted butter
- 1 ½ cups unsweetened cocoa powder
- 1 cup mini semi-sweet chocolate chips

Directions:
1. Place ingredients in the bread machine pan according to the manufacturer's recommended order.
2. Or premix the ingredients in a bowl, mix the liquid ingredients first with a mixer and add in dry ingredients.
3. Use a spatula to fold together everything and transfer the batter to the bread machine pan.

4. Select the Quick/Cake Bread cycle with Light Crust and loaf size on your bread machine, and press Start.
5. When the cake bread is done, unplug the machine and remove the pan.
6. Gently shake the bucket to remove the cake bread, and place it on a cooling rack.
7. Slice after 25 minutes and enjoy!

Nutrition:
Per Serving Calories: 399, Total Fat: 19g, Saturated Fat: 11g, Carbohydrates: 54g, Fiber: 5g, Sodium: 351mg, Protein: 5g

Tip: By pouring a premixed batter into a bread machine will ensure there are no lumps in the end product and the baking is even too.

77. Moist Quick Chocolate Cake

Prep Time: 5 minutes or less
Ready Time: 1 hour

12 Slices/1 ½ pounds
- 2 eggs
- 1 ½ cup sugar
- ⅞ cup milk
- ½ cup cocoa powder
- 3 cups all-purpose flour
- 1 teaspoon baking soda
- 1 ½ teaspoons vanilla extract
- 1 teaspoon baking powder
- ⅞ cup butter, room temperature

16 Slices/2 pounds
- 3 eggs
- 1 ⅔ cup sugar
- 1 cup milk
- 1 cup cocoa powder
- 4 cups all-purpose flour
- 1 ½ teaspoons baking soda
- 2 teaspoons vanilla extract
- 1 ½ teaspoons baking powder
- 1 cup butter, room temperature

Directions:
1. Place all the ingredients in the bread machine pan according to your manufacturer's recommended order.
2. Select the Quick/Cake Bread cycle with loaf size on your bread machine, and press Start.
3. When the cake bread is done, unplug the machine and remove the pan.
4. Put a plate over the bucket and flip over to remove the cake bread or it will fall apart if you take it out by shaking the bucket.
5. Place it on a cooling rack.
6. Slice after 25 minutes and enjoy!

Nutrition:
Per Serving Calories: 397, Total Fat: 19.6g, Saturated Fat: 11.9g, Carbohydrates: 52.3g, Fiber: 1.9g, Sodium: 230mg, Protein: 6.2g

78. Quick Zucchini Bread Loaf

Prep Time: 5 minutes or less
Ready Time: 1 hour 40 minutes

12 Slices/1 ½ pounds
- ⅞ cup sugar
- 3 eggs, beaten
- 1 teaspoon salt
- 1 cup vegetable oil
- 1 teaspoon allspice
- 1 ½ teaspoon cinnamon
- 1 ⅛ teaspoon baking soda
- 3 cups all-purpose flour
- 2 ½ cups shredded zucchini
- 2 ½ teaspoons baking powder

16 Slices/2 pounds
- 1 cup sugar
- 4 eggs, beaten
- 1 ½ teaspoon salt
- 1 ½ cup vegetable oil
- 1 ½ teaspoon allspice
- 2 teaspoons cinnamon
- 1 ¼ teaspoon baking soda
- 4 cups all-purpose flour
- 2 ⅔ cups shredded zucchini
- 3 teaspoons baking powder

Directions:

1. Place all the ingredients except zucchini in the bread machine pan according to your manufacturer's recommended order.
2. Select the Quick/Cake Bread cycle with medium crust and preferable loaf size on your bread machine, and press Start.
3. Allow the machine to start kneading for a few minutes before adding the zucchini, or add when the machine beeps for mix-in ingredients.
4. When the bread is done, unplug the machine and remove the pan.
5. Gently shake the bucket to remove the bread, and place it on a cooling rack.
6. Slice after 25 minutes and enjoy!

Nutrition:

Per Serving Calories: 335, Total Fat: 15.7g, Saturated Fat: 3.2g, Carbohydrates: 44.6g, Fiber: 1.9g, Sodium: 334mg, Protein: 5.7g

Chapter 9: Sweet Bread Recipes

79. Nutty Banana Bread

Prep Time: 10 minutes or less
Ready Time: 3 hours 10 minutes

12 Slices/1 ½ pounds

- 1 teaspoon salt
- 1 ½ teaspoon vanilla paste
- ½ cup pomace olive oil
- 1 ½ teaspoons baking soda
- 3 cups all-purpose flour
- 1 ½ tablespoons chia seeds
- 1 ½ teaspoons baking powder
- 2 ½ tablespoons agave syrup
- 3 medium bananas, mashed
- 2 ½ tablespoons milled flaxseed
- 2 medium eggs, lightly beaten
- 1 cup mixed nuts, roughly chopped

16 Slices/2 pounds

- 1 ½ teaspoons salt
- 2 teaspoons vanilla paste
- 1 cup pomace olive oil
- 2 teaspoons baking soda
- 4 cups all-purpose flour
- 2 tablespoons chia seeds
- 2 teaspoons baking powder
- 3 tablespoons agave syrup
- 4 medium bananas, mashed
- 3 tablespoons milled flaxseed

- 3 medium eggs, lightly beaten
- 1 ½ cup mixed nuts, roughly chopped

Directions:

1. Place ingredients except the nuts and seeds in the bread machine pan according to the manufacturer's recommended order.
2. Add the nuts and seeds during the finishing stages of the kneading cycle.
3. Select the Express Bake cycle or (something equivalent) with Light crust and preferable loaf size on your bread machine, and press Start.

4. When the bread is done, unplug the machine and remove the pan.
5. Gently shake the bucket to remove the bread, and place it on a cooling rack.
6. Slice after 10 minutes and enjoy!

Nutrition:

Per Serving Calories: 269, Total Fat: 8.8g, Saturated Fat: 1.4g, Carbohydrates: 42.5g, Fiber: 4.2g, Sodium: 355mg, Protein: 7.5g

Tip: During the kneading cycle, give the bread a thorough mix once with a spatula or whisk to ensure everything is mixed properly and no add-ins are stuck to the bottom.

80. Date Bread with Cinnamon

Prep Time: 10 minutes or less
Ready Time: 1 hours 10 minute

12 Slices/1 ½ pound

- 1 medium egg
- 1 teaspoon sea salt
- 1 teaspoon cinnamon
- 3 cups all-purpose flour
- 2 tablespoons date syrup
- 1 ½ tablespoons olive oil
- 1 ¾ teaspoons active dry yeast
- ½ cup dates, roughly-chopped
- 2 tablespoons ground flaxseeds
- ⅞ cup coconut or almond milk
- 1 tablespoon plus 2 teaspoons water

16 Slices/2 pounds

- 2 medium egg
- 1 ½ teaspoons sea salt
- 1 ½ teaspoons cinnamon
- 4 cups all-purpose flour
- 2 ½ tablespoons date syrup
- 2 tablespoons olive oil
- 2 teaspoons active dry yeast
- 1 cup dates, roughly-chopped
- 2 ½ tablespoons ground flaxseeds
- 1 cup coconut or almond milk
- 1 ½ tablespoon plus 2 teaspoons water

Directions:

1. Place ingredients except the dates and flax-seeds in the bread machine pan according to the manufacturer's recommended order.
2. Add the dates and flaxseeds during the finishing stages of the kneading cycle.
3. Select the Express Bake cycle or (something equivalent) with Light crust and preferable loaf size on your bread machine, and press Start.
4. When the bread is done, unplug the machine and remove the pan.
5. Gently shake the bucket to remove the bread, and place it on a cooling rack.
6. Slice after 10 minutes and enjoy!

Nutrition:

Per Serving Calories: 214, Total Fat: 7.6g, Saturated Fat: 4.7g, Carbohydrates: 32.5g, Fiber: 2.4g, Sodium: 166mg, Protein: 4.8g

Tip: You can substitute date syrup with muscovado sugar in case of availability issues. If you're allergic to flaxseeds, replace them with chia seeds or simply omit them.

81. Pumpernickel Bread

Prep Time: 10 minutes or less
Ready Time: 3 hours 55 minutes

12 Slices/1 ½ pounds

- ⅓ cup molasses
- 1 cup rye flour
- 1 ½ teaspoons salt
- 3 tablespoons cocoa
- 1 ½ cups bread flour
- 1 ⅛ cups warm water
- 1 cup whole wheat flour
- 1 tablespoon caraway seeds
- 1 ½ tablespoons vegetable oil
- 1 ½ tablespoons vital wheat gluten
- 2 ½ teaspoons bread machine yeast

16 Slices/2 pounds

- ½ cup molasses
- 1 ½ cups rye flour
- 2 teaspoons salt
- 4 tablespoons cocoa
- 2 cups bread flour
- 1 ¼ cups warm water
- 1 ½ cup whole wheat flour
- 1 ½ tablespoons caraway seeds
- 2 tablespoons vegetable oil
- 2 tablespoons vital wheat gluten
- 3 teaspoons bread machine yeast

Directions:

1. Place ingredients in the bread machine pan according to the manufacturer's recommended order.
2. Select the Basic cycle with preferable crust and loaf size on your bread machine, and press Start.
3. When the bread is done, unplug the machine and remove the pan.
4. Gently shake the bucket to remove the bread, and place it on a cooling rack.
5. Slice after 10 minutes and enjoy!

Nutrition:

Per Serving Calories: 119, Total Fat: 2g, Saturated Fat: 0g, Carbohydrates: 22g, Fiber: 3g, Sodium: 295mg, Protein: 3g

Tip: You can ground caraway seeds if you don't want them to stand out in the bread. If you want to make a less dense bread, decrease the whole wheat flour and increase the bread flour amount.

82. Cream Cheese Sweet Bread

Prep Time: 10 minutes or less
Ready Time: 2 hours 50 minutes

12 Slices/1 ½ pounds

- 1 egg
- ⅓ cup milk
- 1 teaspoon salt
- ¼ cup margarine
- ¼ cup dried fruits
- 3 cups bread flour
- 1 cup cream cheese
- 3 tablespoons white sugar
- 2 ½ teaspoons active dry yeast

16 Slices/2 pounds

- 2 eggs
- ½ cup milk
- 1 ½ teaspoons salt
- ⅓ cup margarine
- ⅓ cup dried fruits
- 4 cups bread flour
- 1 ½ cup cream cheese
- 3 ½ tablespoons white sugar
- 2 teaspoons active dry yeast

Directions:

1. Place ingredients except dried fruit in the bread machine pan according to the manufacturer's recommended order.
2. Add dried fruit 10 minutes before the kneading cycle ends.
3. Select the White Bread cycle with Light crust and preferable loaf size on your bread machine, and press Start.
4. When the bread is done, unplug the machine and remove the pan.
5. Gently shake the bucket to remove the bread, and place it on a cooling rack.
6. Slice after 10 minutes and enjoy!

Nutrition:

Per Serving Calories: 248, Total Fat: 12g, Saturated Fat: 5g, Carbohydrates: 29g, Fiber: 1g, Sodium: 305mg, Protein: 7g

Tip: Serve the bread with jam for extra sweetness or simply with coffee or tea.

83. Sweet Fruit Bread

Prep Time: 10 minutes or less
Ready Time: 3 hours 5 minutes

12 Slices/1 ½ pounds

- 1 cup water
- 1 egg, beaten
- ½ cup raisins
- 1 cup bread flour
- 1 ½ teaspoons salt
- 2 tablespoons honey
- 2 cups all-purpose flour
- 2 tablespoons margarine

- 1 teaspoon ground ginger
- ½ teaspoon ground mace
- 1 teaspoon ground nutmeg
- ½ teaspoon ground allspice
- 1 teaspoon ground cinnamon
- 2 tablespoons dry milk powder
- ½ teaspoon ground cardamom
- 1 ¼ teaspoons active dry yeast
- ½ cup candied mixed fruit peel

16 Slices/2 pounds

- 1 ½ cups water
- 2 eggs, beaten
- ¾ cup raisins
- 1 ½ cups bread flour
- 2 teaspoons salt
- 2 ½ tablespoons honey
- 2 ½ cups all-purpose flour
- 2 ½ tablespoons margarine
- 1 ½ teaspoons ground ginger
- 1 teaspoon ground mace
- 1 ½ teaspoons ground nutmeg
- 1 teaspoon ground allspice
- 1 ½ teaspoons ground cinnamon
- 2 ½ tablespoons dry milk powder
- 1 teaspoon ground cardamom
- 1 ½ teaspoons active dry yeast
- 1 cup candied mixed fruit peel

Directions:

1. Place ingredients except fruit peel and raisins in the bread machine pan according to the manufacturer's recommended order.
2. Add fruit peel and raisins 10 minutes before the kneading cycle ends or when the machine beeps for mix-in ingredients.
3. Select the Sweet Bread cycle with preferable crust and loaf size on your bread machine, and press Start.
4. When the bread is done, unplug the machine and remove the pan.
5. Gently shake the bucket to remove the bread, and place it on a cooling rack.
6. Slice after 10 minutes and enjoy!

Nutrition:
Per Serving Calories: 208, Total Fat: 3g, Saturated Fat: 1g, Carbohydrates: 41g, Fiber: 2g, Sodium: 325mg, Protein: 5g

Tip: You can experiment with this recipe by using mixed fruits, cranberries, walnuts, pecans, etc.

84. Cranberry & Oats Bread

Prep Time: 10 minutes or less
Ready Time: 3 hours 40 minutes

12 Slices/1 ½ pounds
- 1 egg
- ¼ cup water
- 1 teaspoon salt
- 3 cups bread flour
- ¼ cups rolled oats
- 3 tablespoons honey
- ½ cup chopped pecans
- ¼ teaspoon baking soda
- ¾ cup dried cranberries
- 2 teaspoons active dry yeast
- ½ teaspoon ground cinnamon
- 1 cup buttermilk, room temperature
- 1 ½ tablespoons margarine, softened

16 Slices/2 pounds
- 2 eggs
- ⅓ cup water
- 1 ½ teaspoons salt
- 4 cups bread flour
- ⅓ cups rolled oats
- 3 ½ tablespoons honey
- 1 cup chopped pecans
- ½ teaspoon baking soda
- ⅞ cup dried cranberries
- 2 ½ teaspoons active dry yeast
- 1 teaspoon ground cinnamon
- 1 ½ cups buttermilk, room temperature
- 2 tablespoons margarine, softened

Directions:
1. Place ingredients except cranberries and pecans in the bread machine pan according to the manufacturer's recommended order.
2. Add cranberries and pecans 10 minutes before the kneading cycle ends or when the machine beeps for mix-in ingredients.
3. Select the Sweet Bread cycle with Light crust and preferable loaf size on your bread machine, and press Start.
4. When the bread is done, unplug the machine and remove the pan.
5. Gently shake the bucket to remove the bread, and place it on a cooling rack.
6. Slice after 10 minutes and enjoy!

Nutrition:
Per Serving Calories: 184, Total Fat: 5g, Saturated Fat: 1g, Carbohydrates: 31g, Fiber: 2g, Sodium: 214mg, Protein: 5g

Tip: You can use regular milk if buttermilk is not available. To enhance the flavor of the bread, a teaspoon of cinnamon would do the job.

85. Applesauce & Oat Bread

Prep Time: 5 minutes or less
Ready Time: 3 hours 5 minutes

12 Slices/1 ½ pounds
- 1 ⅛ teaspoons salt
- ⅓ cup rolled oats
- ¾ cup warm water
- 1 ½ tablespoons butter
- 3 ¼ cups bread flour
- 1 ½ tablespoons white sugar
- ⅓ cup sweetened applesauce
- 1 ½ tablespoons dry milk powder
- 1 teaspoon ground cinnamon
- 2 ½ teaspoons active dry yeast

16 Slices/2 pounds
- 1 ¼ teaspoons salt
- ½ cup rolled oats
- ⅞ cup warm water
- 2 tablespoons butter
- 4 ¼ cups bread flour
- 2 tablespoons white sugar
- ½ cup sweetened applesauce
- 2 tablespoons dry milk powder
- 1 ½ teaspoon ground cinnamon

- 2 ¾ teaspoons active dry yeast

Directions:
1. Place ingredients in the bread machine pan according to the manufacturer's recommended order.
2. Select the Sweet Bread cycle with Light crust and preferable loaf size on your bread machine, and press Start.
3. When the bread is done, unplug the machine and remove the pan.
4. Gently shake the bucket to remove the bread, and place it on a cooling rack.
5. Slice after 10 minutes and enjoy!

Nutrition:
Per Serving Calories: 118, Total Fat: 2g, Saturated Fat: 1g, Carbohydrates: 22g, Fiber: 1g, Sodium: 205mg, Protein: 4g

Tip: You can increase the quantity of applesauce if you would like a stronger flavor.

86. Sweet Orange & Cranberry Bread

Prep Time: 5 minutes or less
Ready Time: 3 hours 5 minutes

12 Slices/1 ½ pounds
- 1 ½ teaspoons salt
- ½ cup warm water
- ¾ cup plain yogurt
- 3 tablespoons honey
- 1 teaspoon orange oil
- 1 cup dried cranberries
- 3 cups all-purpose flour
- 1 tablespoon melted butter
- 2 teaspoons active dry yeast

16 Slices/2 pounds
- 1 ¾ teaspoons salt
- 1 cup warm water
- 1 cup plain yogurt
- 3 ½ tablespoons honey
- 1 ½ teaspoons orange oil
- 1 ½ cup dried cranberries
- 4 cups all-purpose flour
- 1 ½ tablespoons melted butter

- 2 ½ teaspoons active dry yeast

Directions:
1. Place ingredients in the bread machine pan according to the manufacturer's recommended order.
2. Select the Light cycle with preferable loaf size on your bread machine, and press Start.
3. When the bread is done, unplug the machine and remove the pan.
4. Gently shake the bucket to remove the bread, and place it on a cooling rack.
5. Slice after 10 minutes and enjoy!

Nutrition:
Per Serving Calories: 180, Total Fat: 2g, Saturated Fat: 1g, Carbohydrates: 38g, Fiber: 1g, Sodium: 310mg, Protein: 4g

Tip: You can increase the quantity of orange oil if you would like a stronger flavor.

87. Sweet Portuguese Bread

Prep Time: 5 minutes or less
Ready Time: 3 hours 5 minutes

12 Slices/1 ½ pounds
- 1 egg
- 1 cup milk
- ¾ teaspoon salt
- 3 cups bread flour
- ⅓ cup white sugar
- 2 tablespoons margarine
- 2 ½ teaspoons active dry yeast

16 Slices/2 pounds
- 2 eggs
- 1 ½ cup milk
- 1 teaspoon salt
- 4 cups bread flour
- ½ cup white sugar
- 2 ½ tablespoons margarine
- 2 ¾ teaspoons active dry yeast

Directions:
1. Place ingredients in the bread machine pan according to the manufacturer's recommended order.

2. Select the Sweet Bread cycle with preferable crust and loaf size on your bread machine, and press Start.
3. When the bread is done, unplug the machine and remove the pan.
4. Gently shake the bucket to remove the bread, and place it on a cooling rack.
5. Slice after 10 minutes and enjoy!

Nutrition:
Per Serving Calories: 56, Total Fat: 3g, Saturated Fat: 1g, Carbohydrates: 7g, Fiber: 1g, Sodium: 181mg, Protein: 2g

Tip: Serve this bread with jam and tea for the best experience.

88. Sweet Rum Raisin Bread

Prep Time: 5 minutes or less
Ready Time: 2 hours 55 minutes

12 Slices/1 ½ pounds
- 1 egg
- ¾ cup raisins
- ¾ cup water
- 1 ¼ teaspoons salt
- 3 cups bread flour
- 2 ½ teaspoons butter
- 1 ½ teaspoon olive oil
- 2 ½ tablespoons rum
- 2 ½ teaspoons brown sugar
- 1 ½ tablespoon dry milk powder
- 2 teaspoons active dry yeast
- 1 teaspoon rum flavored extract
- 2 ½ tablespoons heavy whipping cream

16 Slices/2 pounds
- 2 eggs
- 1 cup raisins
- 1 cup water
- 1 ½ teaspoons salt
- 4 cups bread flour
- 3 teaspoons butter
- 2 teaspoons olive oil
- 2 tablespoons rum
- 3 teaspoons brown sugar
- 2 tablespoons dry milk powder

- 2 ½ teaspoons active dry yeast
- 1 ½ teaspoons rum flavored extract
- 3 tablespoons heavy whipping cream

Directions:
1. Add rum over the raisins in a small bowl and let it rest for half an hour.
2. Place the other ingredients in the bread machine pan according to the manufacturer's recommended order.
3. Select the Regular Bread cycle with preferable crust and loaf size on your bread machine, and press Start.
4. Add the rum and raisins mixture 10 minutes before the kneading cycle ends, or when the machine beeps for mix-in ingredients (if available.)
5. When the bread is done, unplug the machine and remove the pan.
6. Gently shake the bucket to remove the bread, and place it on a cooling rack.
7. Slice after 10 minutes and enjoy!

Nutrition:
Per Serving Calories: 164, Total Fat: 3g, Saturated Fat: 2g, Carbohydrates: 27g, Fiber: 1g, Sodium: 252mg, Protein: 5g

Tip: If you have time, we recommend soaking the raisins in the rum overnight and using that the next day in the recipe for best results.

89. Sweet & Spicy Fruit Bread

Prep Time: 5 minutes or less
Ready Time: 3 hours 55 minutes

12 Slices/1 ½ pounds
- 1 1/16 cups water
- 3 ¼ cups bread flour
- ¾ cup golden raisins
- 2 tablespoons bread flour
- 2 tablespoons brown sugar
- 2 teaspoons active dry yeast
- 1 ½ tablespoons vegetable oil
- 3 tablespoons dry milk powder
- 1 tablespoon pumpkin pie spice
- 2 ⅔ tablespoons candied mixed fruit peel

16 Slices/2 pounds

- 1 ⅙ cups water
- 4 ¼ cups bread flour
- 1 cup golden raisins
- 2 ½ m tablespoons bread flour
- 2 ½ tablespoons brown sugar
- 2 ½ teaspoons active dry yeast
- 2 tablespoons vegetable oil
- 3 ½ tablespoons dry milk powder
- 1 ½ tablespoon pumpkin pie spice
- 2 ¾ tablespoons candied mixed fruit peel

Directions:

1. Place ingredients except raisins and fruit peel in the bread machine pan according to the manufacturer's recommended order.
2. Add raisins and fruit peel 10 minutes before the kneading cycle ends or when the machine beeps for mix-in ingredients.
3. Select the Fruit Bread cycle (if available) or Basic White Bread with preferable loaf size on your bread machine, and press Start.
4. When the bread is done, unplug the machine and remove the pan.
5. Gently shake the bucket to remove the bread, and place it on a cooling rack.
6. Slice after 10 minutes and enjoy!

Nutrition:

(Per Serving) Calories: 155, Total Fat: 4g, Saturated Fat: 0g, Carbohydrates: 28g, Fiber: 1g, Sodium: 24mg, Protein: 4g

Tip: You can increase the quantity of raisins and brown sugar if you would like a stronger taste.

90. Pecan & Raisin Bread

Prep Time: 10 minutes or less
Ready Time: 3 hours 10 minutes

12 Slices/1 ½ pounds

- 1 egg
- ½ cup raisins
- ½ teaspoon salt
- 3 cups bread flour
- 7 ½ teaspoons butter
- 5 ½ tablespoons sugar

- ½ tablespoon active dry yeast
- ½ cup pecans, finely-chopped
- ⅛ cup nonfat dry milk powder
- ½ cup plus 2 tablespoons water

16 Slices/2 pounds

- 1 egg
- 1 cup raisins
- 1 teaspoon salt
- 4 cups bread flour
- 8 teaspoons butter
- 6 tablespoons sugar
- 1 tablespoon active dry yeast
- 1 cup pecans, finely-chopped
- ¼ cup nonfat dry milk powder
- 1 cup plus 2 tablespoons water

Directions:

1. Place ingredients except raisins in the bread machine pan according to the manufacturer's recommended order.
2. Add raisins 10 minutes before the kneading cycle ends or when the machine beeps for mix-in ingredients.
3. Select the Basic Bread cycle with preferable crust and loaf size on your bread machine, and press Start.
4. When the bread is done, unplug the machine and remove the pan.
5. Gently shake the bucket to remove the bread, and place it on a cooling rack.
6. Slice after 10 minutes and enjoy!

Nutrition:

(Per Serving) Calories: 277, Total Fat: 8g, Saturated Fat: 2g, Carbohydrates: 36g, Fiber: 2g, Sodium: 182mg, Protein: 6g

Tip: You can wrap the bread in foil and store in the freezer. Thaw an hour before use again!

91. Cherry & Pecan Bread

Prep Time: 10 minutes or less
Ready Time: 3 hours 10 minutes

12 Slices/1 ½ pounds
- ⅓ cup water
- 1 teaspoon salt
- 3 cups bread flour
- ½ cup dried cherries
- ½ cup chopped pecans
- ⅔ cup warm whole milk
- ⅓ cup packed brown sugar
- 5 tablespoons baking cocoa
- 5 tablespoons butter, softened
- 2 ¼ teaspoons active dry yeast

16 Slices/2 pounds
- ½ cup water
- 1 ½ teaspoons salt
- 4 cups bread flour
- 1 cup dried cherries
- 1 cup chopped pecans
- ¾ cup warm whole milk
- ½ cup packed brown sugar
- 5 ½ tablespoons baking cocoa
- 5 ½ tablespoons butter, softened
- 2 ½ teaspoons active dry yeast

Directions:
1. Place ingredients except cherries and pecans in the bread machine pan according to the manufacturer's recommended order.
2. Add cherries and pecans 10 minutes before the kneading cycle ends or when the machine beeps for mix-in ingredients.
3. Select the Basic Bread cycle with preferable crust and loaf size on your bread machine, and press Start.
4. When the bread is done, unplug the machine and remove the pan.
5. Gently shake the bucket to remove the bread, and place it on a cooling rack.
6. Slice after 10 minutes and enjoy!

Nutrition:
(Per Serving) Calories: 215, Total Fat: 7.6g, Saturated Fat: 3.6g, Carbohydrates: 33g, Fiber: 2.8g, Sodium: 237mg, Protein: 4.8g

Tip: You can add vanilla and chocolate chips in the bread to enhance its flavor.

Chapter 10: Gluten-Free Bread Recipes

92. Easy Gluten Free Bread

Prep Time: 10 minutes or less
Ready Time: 2 hours 40 minutes

12 Slices/1 ½ pounds
- 2 large eggs
- 1 ¼ teaspoons salt
- 1 ½ cups warm water
- 1 ½ tablespoons white sugar
- 1 ¼ teaspoons cider vinegar
- 2 ¼ teaspoons xanthan gum
- 1 ¼ tablespoon active dry yeast
- 2 tablespoons vegetable oil
- 3 ½ cups gluten free all-purpose flour

16 Slices/2 pounds
- 2 large eggs
- 1 ½ teaspoons salt
- 1 ⅔ cups warm water
- 2 tablespoons white sugar
- 1 ½ teaspoons cider vinegar
- 2 ½ teaspoons xanthan gum
- 1 ½ tablespoon active dry yeast
- 2 ½ tablespoons vegetable oil
- 4 ½ cups gluten free all-purpose flour

Directions:
1. Place ingredients in the bread machine pan according to the manufacturer's recommended order.
2. Select the Basic cycle with Light or Medium crust and preferable loaf size on your bread machine, and press Start.
3. When the bread is done, unplug the machine and remove the pan.
4. Gently shake the bucket to remove the bread, and place it on a cooling rack.
5. Slice after 10 minutes and enjoy!

Nutrition:
Per Serving Calories: 198, Total Fat: 5g, Saturated Fat: 1g, Carbohydrates: 35g, Fiber: 6g, Sodium: 340mg, Protein: 6g

Tip: Always consult your bread machine's manual for setting the timing of the recipes.

93. Healthy Gluten Free Bread

Prep Time: 10 minutes or less
Ready Time: 2 hours 40 minutes

12 Slices/1 ½ pounds
- 1 egg
- ¼ cup honey
- 1 teaspoon salt
- ⅓ cup egg whites
- ¼ cup canola oil
- ¼ cup millet flour
- ½ cup tapioca flour
- 1 cup white rice flour
- 1 cup brown rice flour
- 1 ½ cups warm skim milk
- 1 tablespoon xanthan gum
- ¼ cup garbanzo bean flour
- 1 tablespoon active dry yeast
- 1 tablespoon apple cider vinegar

16 Slices/2 pounds
- 2 eggs
- ½ cup honey
- 1 ½ teaspoons salt
- ½ cup egg whites
- ½ cup canola oil
- ½ cup millet flour
- 1 cup tapioca flour
- 1 ½ cup white rice flour
- 1 ½ cup brown rice flour
- 2 cups warm skim milk
- 1 ½ tablespoon xanthan gum
- ½ cup garbanzo bean flour
- 1 ½ tablespoons active dry yeast
- 1 ½ tablespoon apple cider vinegar

Directions:
1. Place ingredients in the bread machine pan according to the manufacturer's recommended order.
2. Select the cycle with crust and preferable loaf size on your bread machine, and press Start.

3. When the bread is done, unplug the machine and remove the pan.
4. Gently shake the bucket to remove the bread, and place it on a cooling rack.
5. Slice after 10 minutes and enjoy!

Nutrition:
Per Serving Calories: 225, Total Fat: 6g, Saturated Fat: 1g, Carbohydrates: 38g, Fiber: 3g, Sodium: 255mg, Protein: 5g

Tip: You can substitute skim milk with rice milk for an enhanced flavor.

94. Gluten-Free Einkorn-Style Bread

Prep Time: 10 minutes or less
Ready Time: 1 hours 45 minutes

12 Slices/1 ½ pounds
- ¼ cup milk
- 1 ¼ cups water
- ¼ cup gluten free oat flour
- ⅛ cup flax seeds
- 1 ½ cups gluten free all-purpose flour
- 1 teaspoon salt
- 1 ½ cups almond flour
- 1 ½ tablespoons butter
- 1 ½ tablespoons white sugar
- 1 ¾ teaspoons fast-rising yeast

16 Slices/2 pounds
- ⅓ cup milk
- 1 ⅓ cups water
- ½ cup gluten free oat flour
- ¼ cup flax seeds
- 2 cups gluten free all-purpose flour
- 1 ½ teaspoons salt
- 2 cups almond flour
- 2 tablespoons butter
- 2 tablespoons white sugar
- 2 teaspoons fast-rising yeast

Directions:
1. Place ingredients in the bread machine pan according to the manufacturer's recommended order.

2. Select the Wheat cycle with crust and preferable loaf size on your bread machine, and press Start.
3. When the bread is done, unplug the machine and remove the pan.
4. Gently shake the bucket to remove the bread, and place it on a cooling rack.
5. Slice after 10 minutes and enjoy!

Nutrition:
Per Serving Calories: 118, Total Fat: 5g, Saturated Fat: 1g, Carbohydrates: 20g, Fiber: 1g, Sodium: 186mg, Protein: 4g

Tip: You can use oat bran instead of oat flour for a different take. If your dough calls for more milk, add more.

95. Whole Grain Gluten Free Bread

Prep Time: 10 minutes or less
Ready Time: 3 hours 50 minutes

12 Slices/1 ½ pounds
- 2 large eggs
- ⅓ cup teff flour
- 1 ¼ cup cornstarch
- 1 cup millet flour
- ½ cup ground flax
- 1 ¾ teaspoons salt
- ¾ cup milk powder
- 1 ¾ cups warm water
- ½ cup tapioca starch
- ¼ cup sweet rice flour
- 3 tablespoons canola oil
- 1 teaspoon white vinegar
- 2 ½ teaspoons guar gum
- 3 tablespoons white sugar
- 2 tablespoons psyllium husk
- 2 ¾ teaspoons active dry yeast

16 Slices/2 pounds
- 3 large eggs
- ½ cup teff flour
- 1 ½ cup cornstarch
- 1 ½ cup millet flour
- 1 cup ground flax
- 2 teaspoons salt

- ⅞ cup milk powder
- 1 ⅞ cups warm water
- 1 cup tapioca starch
- ½ cup sweet rice flour
- 3 ½ tablespoons canola oil
- 1 ½ teaspoons white vinegar
- 3 teaspoons guar gum
- 3 ½ tablespoons white sugar
- 2 ½ tablespoons psyllium husk
- 3 teaspoons active dry yeast

Directions:
1. Place ingredients in the bread machine pan according to the manufacturer's recommended order.
2. Select the Rapid Bake cycle with Dark crust and preferable loaf size on your bread machine, and press Start.
3. When the bread is done, unplug the machine and remove the pan.
4. Gently shake the bucket to remove the bread, and place it on a cooling rack.
5. Slice after 10 minutes and enjoy!

Nutrition:
Per Serving Calories: 238, Total Fat: 7g, Saturated Fat: 1g, Carbohydrates: 39g, Fiber: 3g, Sodium: 400mg, Protein: 6g

Tip: Once you add the ingredients in the pan, give it a good mix with a wooden spoon to make sure everything is properly mixed, specifically yeast!

96. Raisin Bran Bread Loaf

Prep Time: 10 minutes or less
Ready Time: 3 hours 10 minutes

12 Slices/1 ½ pounds
- 1 ¾ cups water
- 3 cups gluten free bread flour
- 1 ¼ teaspoons salt
- 1 ½ tablespoons white sugar
- 1 ½ teaspoons active dry yeast
- 2 ½ cups raisin bran bread cereal

16 Slices/2 pounds
- 2 cups water

- 4 cups gluten free bread flour
- 1 ½ teaspoons salt
- 2 tablespoons white sugar
- 2 teaspoons active dry yeast
- 3 ½ cups raisin bran bread cereal

Directions:
1. Place ingredients in the bread machine pan according to the manufacturer's recommended order.
2. Select the Medium crust cycle and preferable loaf size on your bread machine, and press Start.
3. When the bread is done, unplug the machine and remove the pan.
4. Gently shake the bucket to remove the bread, and place it on a cooling rack.
5. Slice after 10 minutes and enjoy!

Nutrition:
Per Serving Calories: 153, Total Fat: 1g, Saturated Fat: 0g, Carbohydrates: 32g, Fiber: 2g, Sodium: 240mg, Protein: 5g

Tip: You can add cinnamon to the bread for enhanced flavor.

97. Gluten Free White Bread

Prep Time: 10 minutes or less
Ready Time: 3 hours 10 minutes

12 Slices/1 ½ pounds
- 2 eggs
- ¼ cup honey
- ¼ cup olive oil
- 1 teaspoon salt
- ½ cup soy flour
- ⅓ cup cornstarch
- ½ cup potato starch
- 2 cups white rice flour
- 1 tablespoon xanthan gum
- 1 tablespoon cider vinegar
- 1 tablespoon active dry yeast
- 1 ½ cups buttermilk, room temperature

16 Slices/2 pounds
- 3 eggs

- ½ cup honey
- ½ cup olive oil
- 1 ½ teaspoons salt
- 1 cup soy flour
- ½ cup cornstarch
- 1 cup potato starch
- 3 cups white rice flour
- 1 ½ tablespoons xanthan gum
- 1 ½ tablespoon cider vinegar
- 1 ½ tablespoons active dry yeast
- 2 cups buttermilk, room temperature

Directions:

1. Place ingredients in the bread machine pan according to the manufacturer's recommended order.
2. Select the Sweet Dough cycle and preferable loaf size on your bread machine, and press Start.
3. When the bread is done, unplug the machine and remove the pan.
4. Gently shake the bucket to remove the bread, and place it on a cooling rack.
5. Slice after 10 minutes and enjoy!

Nutrition:

Per Serving Calories: 242, Total Fat: 7g, Saturated Fat: 1g, Carbohydrates: 40g, Fiber: 3g, Sodium: 275mg, Protein: 6g

Tip: You can add more flour and milk to balance the dough texture. It should always be smooth!

98. Gluten Free Almond Bread

Prep Time: 15 minutes or less
Ready Time: 3 hours 15 minutes

12 Slices/1 ½ pounds

- ¼ cup flax meal
- ¼ cup coconut oil
- ½ cup almond milk
- 2 cups almond flour
- ⅓ cup coconut flour
- 1 teaspoon real salt
- 1 tablespoon flax meal
- 1 ½ cups tapioca flour
- 1 teaspoon baking soda

- 4 tablespoons chia seeds
- 3 eggs room temperature
- 2 teaspoon cream of tartar
- ¾ cup plus 1 tablespoon water
- 2 teaspoon bread machine yeast
- 1 tablespoon maple syrup or honey

16 Slices/2 pounds

- ½ cup flax meal
- ½ cup coconut oil
- 1 cup almond milk
- 2 ½ cups almond flour
- ½ cup coconut flour
- 1 ½ teaspoons real salt
- 1 ½ tablespoons flax meal
- 1 ¾ cups tapioca flour
- 1 ½ teaspoons baking soda
- 4 ½ tablespoons chia seeds
- 3 eggs room temperature
- 2 ½ teaspoon cream of tartar
- ⅞ cup plus 1 tablespoon water
- 2 ½ teaspoons bread machine yeast
- 1 ½ tablespoons maple syrup or honey

Directions:

1. Mix chia seeds and flax meal with water and put aside. The mixture will obtain a gel-like consistency in a few minutes and the seeds will thicken.
2. Meanwhile, melt the coconut oil and let it cool down, and mix in eggs, almond milk, honey or maple syrup using a whisk.
3. Mix the honey mixture with chia flax mixture and add it all to the bread machine pan.
4. Add the remaining ingredients to the pan except yeast.
5. Make a small dent in the dry ingredients in the pan and add in yeast.
6. Select the Whole Grain cycle with Light or Dark crust and preferable loaf size on your bread machine, and press Start.
7. When the bread is done, unplug the machine and remove the pan.
8. Gently shake the bucket to remove the bread, and place it on a cooling rack.
9. Slice after 10 minutes and enjoy!

Nutrition:
Per Serving Calories: 114, Total Fat: 6.3g, Saturated Fat: 1g, Carbohydrates: 8g, Fiber: 4.1g, Sodium: 236mg, Protein: 6g

Tip: Serve this bread with honey or butter with a drizzle of cinnamon on top for the best experience!

99. Simple Gluten Free Bread

Prep Time: 15 minutes or less
Ready Time: 4 hours 20 minutes

12 Slices/1 ½ pounds

- 2 large eggs
- 1 ¼ teaspoons salt
- ½ cup olive oil
- ¾ teaspoon gelatin
- ¼ cup organic honey
- 2 ½ teaspoons xanthan gum
- 1 ½ teaspoons baking powder
- 2 ¼ teaspoons active dry yeast
- 1 ⅔ cups warm water or milk
- 1 teaspoon apple cider vinegar
- 3 ½ cups gluten free flour blend

16 Slices/2 pounds

- 3 large eggs
- 1 ½ teaspoons salt
- 1 cup olive oil
- 1 teaspoon gelatin
- ½ cup organic honey
- 3 teaspoons xanthan gum
- 2 teaspoons baking powder
- 2 ½ teaspoons active dry yeast
- 1 ¾ cups warm water or milk
- 1 ½ teaspoon apple cider vinegar
- 4 ½ cups gluten free flour blend

Directions:

1. Place ingredients in the bread machine pan according to the manufacturer's recommended order.
2. Select the Gluten Free cycle with preferable crust and loaf size on your bread machine, and press Start.

3. When the bread is done, unplug the machine and remove the pan.
4. Gently shake the bucket to remove the bread, and place it on a cooling rack.
5. Slice after 10 minutes and enjoy!

Nutrition:
Per Serving Calories: 150, Total Fat: 6g, Saturated Fat: 1g, Carbohydrates: 22g, Fiber: 3g, Sodium: 221mg, Protein: 4g

Tip: Keep a check on the dough while kneading as you can add more flour, water or milk according to its texture. For a darker, crustier top, brush the top with egg wash before baking.

100. Oat Rice Gluten Free Bread

Prep Time: 10 minutes or less
Ready Time: 1 hours 40 minutes

12 Slices/1 ½ pounds

- 3 large eggs
- 1 ⅔ cups water
- ½ cup tapioca flour
- ⅓ cup potato starch
- 1 ½ cups brown rice flour
- 1 ½ teaspoons lemon juice
- 4 ½ teaspoons clear honey
- 1 ½ tablespoons caster sugar
- 1 ¾ teaspoons fine sea salt
- 1 ½ cups gluten free oat flour
- 1 ½ tablespoons xanthan gum
- 4 ½ tablespoons sunflower oil
- 4 ½ tablespoons dried milk powder
- 1 ½ teaspoons easy bake dried yeast

16 Slices/2 pounds

- 4 large eggs
- 1 ¾ cups water
- 1 cup tapioca flour
- ½ cup potato starch
- 2 cups brown rice flour
- 1 ⅔ teaspoons lemon juice
- 4 ¾ teaspoons clear honey
- 2 tablespoons caster sugar
- 2 teaspoons fine sea salt
- 2 cups gluten free oat flour

- 2 tablespoons xanthan gum
- 5 tablespoons sunflower oil
- 5 tablespoons dried milk powder
- 2 teaspoons easy bake dried yeast

Directions:
1. Place ingredients in the bread machine pan according to the manufacturer's recommended order.
2. Select the Basic cycle with Medium crust and preferable loaf size on your bread machine, and press Start.
3. When the bread is done, unplug the machine and remove the pan.
4. Gently shake the bucket to remove the bread, and place it on a cooling rack.
5. Slice after 10 minutes and enjoy!

Nutrition:
Per Serving Calories: 182, Total Fat: 6g, Saturated Fat: 1g, Carbohydrates: 26g, Fiber: 2g, Sodium: 303mg, Protein: 5g

Tip: Don't eat the bread when it's hot. Gluten free breads taste better when they are cold.

101. Vegan Bread Machine Loaf

Prep Time: 10 minutes or less
Ready Time: 1 hours 50 minutes

12 Slices/1 ½ pounds
- ⅓ cup potato starch
- 1 ⅓ dairy free milk
- 1 cup sorghum flour
- 1 ¼ teaspoons fine sea salt
- 1 ¼ teaspoons lemon juice
- 1 cup hot boiled water
- ¾ cup tapioca starch flour
- 2 ½ tablespoons sunflower oil
- 1 ½ cups gluten free oat flour
- ⅓ cup ground psyllium husk
- 2 ½ tablespoons milled flax seed
- 2 ½ teaspoons bicarbonate of soda
- 2 ¼ teaspoons instant bake fast yeast
- 1 ½ tablespoons honey or maple syrup

16 Slices/2 pounds
- ½ cup potato starch
- 1 ½ cups dairy free milk
- 1 ½ cups sorghum flour
- 1 ½ teaspoons fine sea salt
- 1 ½ teaspoons lemon juice
- 1 ½ cups hot boiled water
- 1 cup tapioca starch flour
- 3 tablespoons sunflower oil
- 2 cups gluten free oat flour
- ½ cup ground psyllium husk
- 2 tablespoons milled flax seed
- 2 ¾ teaspoons bicarbonate of soda
- 2 ½ teaspoons instant bake fast yeast
- 2 tablespoons honey or maple syrup

Directions:
1. Place ingredients in the bread machine pan according to the manufacturer's recommended order.
2. Select the GF (or something equipment) cycle with Medium crust and preferable loaf size on your bread machine, and press Start.
3. When the bread is done, unplug the machine and remove the pan.
4. Gently shake the bucket to remove the bread, and place it on a cooling rack.
5. Slice after 10 minutes and enjoy!

Nutrition:
Per Serving Calories: 140, Total Fat:22g, Saturated Fat: 0g, Carbohydrates: 26g, Fiber: 3g, Sodium: 397mg, Protein: 3g

Tip: You can substitute dairy free milk with any type for your personal preference.

102. Linseed Gluten Free Bread

Prep Time: 10 minutes or less
Ready Time: 1 hours 10 minutes

12 Slices/1 ½ pounds

- 1 large egg
- 1 ¾ cups water
- 1 ¾ teaspoons salt
- 1 cup quinoa flour
- 1 ½ tablespoons linseed
- 1 ½ teaspoons lemon juice
- 1 cup buckwheat flour
- 1 ½ cups brown rice flour
- 1 ½ tablespoons black treacle
- 3 ½ tablespoons sunflower oil
- 1 ½ tablespoons xanthan gum
- 1 ½ tablespoons active dried yeast
- 2 ½ teaspoons light brown sugar
- 3 ½ tablespoons dry milk powder
- 1 ½ tablespoons gluten-free baking powder

16 Slices/2 pounds

- 2 large eggs
- 2 cups water
- 2 teaspoons salt
- 1 ½ cup quinoa flour
- 2 tablespoons linseed
- 2 teaspoons lemon juice
- 1 ½ cup buckwheat flour
- 2 cups brown rice flour
- 2 tablespoons black treacle
- 4 tablespoons sunflower oil
- 2 tablespoons xanthan gum
- 2 tablespoons active dried yeast
- 3 teaspoons light brown sugar
- 4 tablespoons dry milk powder
- 2 tablespoons gluten-free baking powder

Directions:

1. Place ingredients in the bread machine pan according to the manufacturer's recommended order.
2. Select the Basic setting with Medium crust and preferable loaf size on your bread machine, and press Start.
3. When the bread is done, unplug the machine and remove the pan.
4. Gently shake the bucket to remove the bread, and place it on a cooling rack.
5. Slice after 10 minutes and enjoy!

Nutrition:

Per Serving Calories: 292, Total Fat:11.7g, Saturated Fat: 1.3g, Carbohydrates: 50g, Fiber: 18.4g, Sodium: 1190mg, Protein: 9.2g

Tip: You can substitute dry milk with 4 tablespoons of liquid milk in case of availability issues.

103. Cornbread Gluten Free Loaf

Prep Time: 5 minutes or less
Ready Time: 1 hours 5 minutes

12 Slices/1 ½ pounds

- 3 large eggs
- 1 ½ cups milk
- 1 ⅔ teaspoons salt
- 1 ½ tablespoons lemon juice
- 1 ½ cup melted white vegetable fat
- 3 cups plus 2 tablespoons maize flour
- 1 ½ tablespoon gluten free baking powder

16 Slices/2 pounds

- 4 large eggs
- 2 cups milk
- 2 teaspoons salt
- 2 tablespoons lemon juice
- 2 cups melted white vegetable fat
- 4 cups plus 2 tablespoons maize flour
- 2 tablespoons gluten free baking powder

Directions:

1. Place ingredients in the bread machine pan according to the manufacturer's recommended order.
2. Select the Extra Bake setting or (something equivalent) with Medium crust and preferable loaf size on your bread machine, and press Start.
3. When the bread is done, unplug the machine and remove the pan.
4. Gently shake the bucket to remove the bread, and place it on a cooling rack.

5. Slice after 10 minutes and enjoy!

Nutrition:

Per Serving Calories: 468, Total Fat:36.7g, Saturated Fat: 3.6g, Carbohydrates: 82g, Fiber: 48g, Sodium: 619mg, Protein: 3.6g

Tip: When your ingredients are in the dough cycle, use a spatula to give a good mix so that the ingredients won't stick to the bottom to ensure even baking.

104. Rice Gluten Free Bread

Prep Time: 5 minutes or less
Ready Time: 3 hours 15 minutes

12 Slices/1 ½ pounds

- 2 eggs
- 1 ½ cups water
- ½ cup soy milk
- 1 ½ teaspoons salt
- 4 ½ tablespoons oil
- 2 cups rice flour
- 2 ½ tablespoons sugar
- 1 cup brown rice flour
- 1 ½ teaspoon apple cider vinegar
- 2 ¼ teaspoons bread machine yeast
- 1 ⅔ teaspoons xanthan gum or guar guar

16 Slices/2 pounds

- 3 eggs
- 2 cups water
- 1 cup soy milk
- 1 ⅔ teaspoons salt
- 5 tablespoons oil
- 2 ½ cups rice flour
- 3 tablespoons sugar
- 1 ½ cups brown rice flour
- 2 teaspoons apple cider vinegar
- 2 ½ teaspoons bread machine yeast
- 2 ½ teaspoons xanthan gum or guar guar

Directions:

1. Place ingredients in the bread machine pan according to the manufacturer's recommended order.
2. Select the Basic Bread setting with Medium crust and preferable loaf size on your bread machine, and press Start.
3. When the bread is done, unplug the machine and remove the pan.
4. Gently shake the bucket to remove the bread, and place it on a cooling rack.
5. Slice after 10 minutes and enjoy!

Nutrition:

Per Serving Calories: 210, Total Fat: 7.5g, Saturated Fat: 1.4g, Carbohydrates: 31g, Fiber: 1.7g, Sodium: 252mg, Protein: 4.7g

Tip: You can substitute soy milk with skim milk and bread machine yeast with instant yeast in case of availability issues.

Chapter 11: Pizza & Focaccia Bread Recipes

105. Simple Pizza Bread Machine Dough

Prep Time: 10 minutes or less
Ready Time: 1 hour 27 minutes

12 Slices/1 ½ pounds

- 3 cups bread flour
- 1 tablespoon honey
- 1 teaspoon table salt
- 2 tablespoons olive oil
- 1 teaspoon granulated sugar
- 2 teaspoons bread machine yeast
- 1 cup plus 1 tablespoon spring water

16 Slices/2 pounds

- 4 cups bread flour
- 1 ½ tablespoons honey
- 1 ½ teaspoons table salt
- 2 ½ tablespoons olive oil
- 1 ½ teaspoon granulated sugar
- 2 ½ teaspoons bread machine yeast
- 1 ¼ cups spring water

Directions:

1. Place the ingredients in the bread machine pan according to the manufacturer's recommended order.
2. Select the Dough Cycle on your bread machine, and press Start.
3. Keep a check on your dough to see if it needs more flour or water.
4. Meanwhile, preheat the oven at 500 degrees F.
5. Once the dough is done and doubled in size, take it out of the bread machine pan and place on a floured surface.
6. Divide the dough into 2 pieces and shape them one by one into a ball.
7. Cover the balls and let them rest for 10 to 15 minutes to rise once more.
8. Meanwhile grease the pizza pans or baking sheet with oil.
9. Take the dough balls and use your hands to flatten them into a round of your desired thinness, or use a rolling pin.
10. Spread sauce over your pizza, followed with cheese, meat, vegetables and other toppings.
11. Before you put the pizza to bake in the oven, turn down the temperature to 450 F.
12. Bake them for 10 to 15 minutes until the cheese has melted and it all looks golden-brown.
13. Once done, take out the pizza and slice to serve.

Nutrition:
Per Serving Calories: 220, Total Fat: 5g, Saturated Fat: 1g, Carbohydrates: 38g, Fiber: 2g, Sodium: 295mg, Protein: 7g

Tip: You can substitute bread machine yeast with instant yeast or active dry yeast in case of availability issues.

106. Super Easy Pizza Bread

Prep Time: 10 minutes or less
Ready Time: 30 minutes

12 Slices/1 ½ pounds

- 1 teaspoon salt
- 3 cups bread flour
- 2 tablespoons olive oil
- 1 teaspoon granulated sugar
- 2 ½ teaspoon active dry yeast
- 1 cup plus 2 tablespoons water

16 Slices/2 pounds

- 1 ½ teaspoons salt
- 3 cups bread flour
- 3 tablespoons olive oil
- 1 ½ teaspoon granulated sugar
- 2 ¾ teaspoon active dry yeast
- 1 ½ cup water

Directions:

1. Place the ingredients in the bread machine pan according to the manufacturer's recommended order.
2. Select the Dough Cycle on your bread machine, and press Start.

3. Keep a check on your dough to see if it needs more flour or water.
4. Meanwhile preheat the oven at 400 degree F and move the rack to the lowest position.
5. Once the dough is done and doubled in size, take it out of the bread machine pan and place on a floured surface.
6. Divide the dough into 2 pieces and shape them one by one into a ball.
7. Cover the balls and let them rest for 10 to 15 minutes to rise once more.
8. Meanwhile grease the pizza pans or baking sheet with oil.
9. Take the dough balls and use your floured fingers to flatten them into a 12" round of your desired thinness, or use a rolling pin.
10. Spread sauce over your pizza, followed with cheese, meat, vegetables and other toppings.
11. Bake in the oven for 15 to 20 minutes or until perfectly golden-brown at 425 degrees.
12. Once done, take out the pizza and slice to serve.

Nutrition:
Per Serving Calories: 220, Total Fat: 5g, Saturated Fat: 1g, Carbohydrates: 38g, Fiber: 2g, Sodium: 295mg, Protein: 7g

Tip: You can substitute active dry yeast with instant yeast or bread machine yeast and olive oil with vegetable oil in case of availability issues.

107. Sourdough Pizza Dough Bread

Prep Time: 10 minutes or less
Ready Time: 2 hours 5 minutes

12 Slices/1 ½ pounds
- ¾ cup water
- 1 teaspoon salt
- 1 tablespoon sugar
- 3 ½ cups bread flour
- 2 tablespoons olive oil
- 1 teaspoon instant yeast
- ¾ cup sourdough starter
- 1 tablespoon vital wheat gluten

16 Slices/2 pounds
- 1 cup water
- 1 ½ teaspoons salt
- 1 ½ tablespoons sugar
- 4 ½ cups bread flour
- 2 ½ tablespoons olive oil
- 1 ½ teaspoons instant yeast
- 1 cup sourdough starter
- 1 ½ tablespoons vital wheat gluten

Directions:
1. Place the ingredients in the bread machine pan according to the manufacturer's recommended order.
2. Select the Dough Cycle on your bread machine, and press Start.
3. Keep a check on your dough to see if it needs more flour or water.
4. Once the dough is done, knead and put the dough in a greased bowl and let it rise covered at room temperature or in the fridge overnight.
5. Divide the dough into 2 pieces and shape them one by one into a ball.
6. Flatten them into pies and cover with your favorite sauces and toppings.
7. Bake it on preheated stone for 14 to 16 minutes at 475 degree F in the oven.
8. Once done, take out the pizza and slice to serve.

Nutrition:
Per Serving Calories: 945, Total Fat: 15.7g, Saturated Fat: 2.2g, Carbohydrates: 174g, Fiber: 6.3g, Sodium: 170.2mg, Protein: 23.4g

Tip: You can also freeze the oiled dough in a freezer bag for use later. For later, thaw it at room temperature, give it a second rise, and bake as normal.

108. Sparkling Water Pizza Dough

Prep Time: 10 minutes or less
Ready Time: 35 minutes

12 Slices/1 ½ pounds
- ½ teaspoon salt
- ¼ teaspoon sugar
- 3 cups bread flour
- ½ teaspoon rosemary
- ¼ teaspoon cinnamon
- 1 cup sparkling water
- ¼ teaspoon garlic powder
- 1 ½ tablespoons extra virgin olive oil
- ½ teaspoon fast-rising dry active yeast

16 Slices/2 pounds
- 1 teaspoon salt
- ½ teaspoon sugar
- 4 cups bread flour
- 1 teaspoon rosemary
- ½ teaspoon cinnamon
- 1 ¼ cups sparkling water
- ½ teaspoon garlic powder
- 2 tablespoons extra virgin olive oil
- 1 teaspoon fast-rising dry active yeast

Directions:
1. Place the ingredients in the bread machine pan according to the manufacturer's recommended order.
2. Select the Dough Cycle on your bread machine, and press Start.
3. Keep a check on your dough to see if it needs more flour or water.
4. Once the dough is done and doubled in size, take it out of the bread machine pan and place on a floured surface.
5. Divide the dough into 2 pieces and shape them one by one into a ball.
6. Meanwhile grease the pizza pans or baking sheet with oil.
7. Take the dough balls and use your floured fingers to flatten them into a 12" round of your desired thinness, or use a rolling pin.
8. Spread sauce over your pizza, followed with your favorite toppings.
9. Bake for 15 to 20 minutes or until perfectly golden-brown in a preheated oven at 425 degrees.
10. Once done, take out the pizza and slice to serve.

Nutrition:
Per Serving Calories: 263, Total Fat: 4.1g, Saturated Fat: 0.6g, Carbohydrates: 48.6g, Fiber: 2g, Sodium: 292mg, Protein: 7.1g

Tip: Real garlic can kill the yeast, so only use the powdered one. Also, sparkling water can be substituted with tap water for ease.

109. Italian Pizza Crust

Prep Time: 5 minutes or less
Ready Time: 2 hours

12 Slices/1 ½ pounds
- 1 ½ cups water
- 1 teaspoon salt
- 1 tablespoon sugar
- 3 ½ cups plain flour
- 1 ½ tablespoons olive oil
- 1 crushed garlic clove
- 1 ½ tablespoons dry yeast
- 2 ½ teaspoons mixed Italian herbs
- 1 ½ tablespoons grated parmesan cheese

16 Slices/2 pounds
- 2 cups water
- 1 ⅛ teaspoon salt
- 1 ½ tablespoons sugar
- 4 ½ cups plain flour
- 2 tablespoons olive oil
- 1 crushed garlic clove
- 2 tablespoons dry yeast
- 3 teaspoons mixed Italian herbs
- 2 tablespoons grated parmesan cheese

Directions:
1. Place the ingredients in the bread machine pan according to the manufacturer's recommended order.
2. Select the Dough Cycle on your bread machine, and press Start.

3. When done, divide the dough into three and spread into three circles on a baking sheet.
4. Top with your favorite sauces and toppings and bake for 20 minutes or until golden-brown at 180 degrees C.
5. Take out once done and slice to serve.

Nutrition:
Per Serving Calories: 440, Total Fat: 6.3g, Saturated Fat: 1.1g, Carbohydrates: 81.2g, Fiber: 3.9g, Sodium: 32.2mg, Protein: 13.1g

Tip: Use ½ cup flour to add to the dough if it's too sticky.

110. Rosemary & Garlic Focaccia

Prep Time: 5 minutes or less
Ready Time: 2 hours 24 minutes

12 Slices/1 ½ pounds
- 4 garlic cloves
- 1 ¼ cups water
- 1 cup bread flour
- 4 teaspoons yeast
- 1 ½ teaspoons honey
- 7 tablespoons olive oil
- 2 teaspoons rosemary
- 1 ½ teaspoons sea salt
- 2 cups whole wheat flour
- 8 teaspoons minced basil
- 1 ½ tablespoons powdered milk

16 Slices/2 pounds
- 4 ½ garlic cloves
- 1 ½ cups water
- 1 ½ cup bread flour
- 4 ½ teaspoons yeast
- 2 teaspoons honey
- 7 ½ tablespoons olive oil
- 2 ½ teaspoons rosemary
- 2 teaspoons sea salt
- 2 ½ cups whole wheat flour
- 8 ½ teaspoons minced basil
- 2 tablespoons powdered milk

Directions:

1. Place the ingredients in the bread machine pan according to the manufacturer's recommended order but only add 2 crushed garlic cloves.
2. Select the Whole Wheat Dough Cycle on your bread machine, and press Start.
3. When done, divide the dough into three and cover to let it rise for 10 minutes.
4. Crush the other two garlic and mix with the herbs, some salt and ¼ cup oil.
5. Grease two round pans and brush the dough with garlic oil.
6. Bake for 18 to 24 minutes or until golden-brown in a preheated oven at the bottom third place at 400 degrees.
7. Take out once done and slice to serve.

Nutrition:
Per Serving Calories: 1135, Total Fat: 53.2g, Saturated Fat: 8.2g, Carbohydrates: 146.2g, Fiber: 17g, Sodium: 1781mg, Protein: 27.6g

Tip: If you are not in favor of whole wheat flour or want a less dense bread, use all-purpose flour.

111. Herb Focaccia Bread

Prep Time: 5 minutes or less
Ready Time: 3 hours

12 Slices/1 ½ pounds
- ½ cup olive oil
- 2 ¼ teaspoons yeast
- 1 ¾ teaspoons salt
- 1 ½ tablespoon olive oil
- 1 ½ teaspoons dried basil
- 1 ⅛ cup lukewarm water
- ½ teaspoon coarse salt
- 3 ½ cups all-purpose flour

16 Slices/2 pounds
- 1 cup olive oil
- 2 ½ teaspoons yeast
- 2 teaspoons salt
- 2 tablespoons olive oil
- 2 teaspoons dried basil
- 1 ¼ cup lukewarm water
- 1 teaspoon coarse salt

- 4 ½ cups all-purpose flour

Directions:
1. Place the ingredients in the bread machine pan according to the manufacturer's recommended order but only add 2 crushed garlic cloves.
2. Select the Dough Cycle on your bread machine.
3. Keep check on the dough, it should be soft and sticky, and you can adjust it with extra flour or water.
4. Once the dough is done, take it out of the bread machine pan and place on a lightly floured surface.
5. Turn it into a rectangular shape of 17 x 12 inches by using your hands.
6. Grease a cookie sheet and transfer the dough on it.
7. Let it be for 10 minutes and then pat it back into shape.
8. Sprinkle salt, herbs and olive oil over the dough and bake for 15 minutes at 425 degrees.
9. Take out once done and cool on a cooling rack.

Nutrition:
Per Serving Calories: 1988, Total Fat: 90.3g, Saturated Fat: 12.5g, Carbohydrates: 252g, Fiber: 15.2g, Sodium: 4097mg, Protein: 42.1g

Tip: Try this recipe with the addition of roasted red pepper and diced onion.

112. Sun-Dried Tomato Focaccia Bread

Prep Time: 5 minutes or less
Ready Time: 2 hours 30 minutes

12 Slices/1 ½ pounds
- 1 cup water
- 1 teaspoon salt
- 3 cups bread flour
- 1 teaspoon garlic salt
- 2 tablespoons olive oil
- 3 tablespoons margarine
- 2 teaspoons active dry yeast
- 2 tablespoons powdered milk

- 3 ½ tablespoons white sugar
- 2 tablespoons parmesan cheese
- 1 cup shredded mozzarella cheese
- ½ cup chopped sun-dried tomato
- 2 teaspoons crushed dried rosemary

16 Slices/2 pounds
- 1 ½ cups water
- 1 ½ teaspoons salt
- 4 cups bread flour
- 1 ⅛ teaspoon garlic salt
- 2 ½ tablespoons olive oil
- 3 ½ tablespoons margarine
- 2 ½ teaspoons active dry yeast
- 2 ½ tablespoons powdered milk
- 4 tablespoons white sugar
- 2 ½ tablespoons parmesan cheese
- 1 ½ cups shredded mozzarella cheese
- 1 cup chopped sun-dried tomato
- 2 ½ teaspoons crushed dried rosemary

Directions:
1. Add water, flour, milk sugar, salt, margarine, tomatoes, and yeast into the bread machine pan according to the manufacturer's recommended order.
2. Choose the Dough Cycle and Start.
3. Take out the dough once done and knead for a minute.
4. Put the dough in a greased bowl and turn it a few times in the bowl so that it gets covered with oil.
5. Cover with a damp cloth to let it rise for 15 minutes in a warm location.
6. Spread the dough to fit the baking pan and use your fingertips to make indentations.
7. Apply oil over the top surface and cover again with the damp cloth.
8. Let it rise for half an hour and top with cheese, rosemary, garlic salt, and mozzarella.
9. Bake for 15 minutes at 400 degrees F or until golden-brown.
10. Take out the bread when done, cool slightly and slice to serve.

Nutrition:

Per Serving Calories: 441, Total Fat: 16.4g, Saturated Fat: 5.2g, Carbohydrates: 60.3g, Fiber: 2.8g, Sodium: 704mg, Protein: 13.3g

Tip: You can add chives, thyme and basil in this recipe to enhance the flavor.

113. Onion & Cheese Focaccia

Prep Time: 5 minutes or less
Ready Time: 1 hours 18 minutes

12 Slices/1 ½ pounds
- ½ cup butter
- 1 ½ teaspoons salt
- 3 cups bread flour
- 1 ½ tablespoons sugar
- 1 cup warm water
- 2 ½ tablespoons olive oil
- 3 ½ minced garlic cloves
- 2 ½ teaspoons Italian seasoning
- 2 teaspoons active dry yeast
- 1 ½ cups shredded cheddar cheese
- 2 ½ tablespoons grated parmesan cheese
- 2 medium onions, sliced and quartered

16 Slices/2 pounds
- 1 cup butter
- 1 ¾ teaspoons salt
- 4 cups bread flour
- 2 tablespoons sugar
- 1 ½ cups warm water
- 3 tablespoons olive oil
- 4 minced garlic cloves
- 3 teaspoons Italian seasoning
- 2 ¾ teaspoons active dry yeast
- 2 cups shredded cheddar cheese
- 3 tablespoons grated parmesan cheese
- 3 medium onions, sliced and quartered

Directions:
1. Add water, flour, sugar, oil, salt and yeast into the bread machine pan according to the manufacturer's recommended order.
2. Choose the Dough Cycle and Start.
3. Keep check on the dough, it should be soft and sticky, and you can adjust it with extra flour or water.
4. Put the dough in a greased 12" pizza pan and pat into a 10" circle.
5. Cover with a damp cloth to let it rise for 30 minutes in a warm location.
6. Meanwhile, cook minced garlic in a pan and mix in Italian seasoning.
7. Use a wooden spoon to make indentations in the dough and cover with onion and cheese.
8. Bake for 15 to 20 or until golden-brown at 400 degrees F.
9. Take out the bread when done, cool slightly and slice to serve.

Nutrition:
Per Serving Calories: 370, Total Fat: 19.4g, Saturated Fat: 9.8g, Carbohydrates: 38g, Fiber: 2g, Sodium: 601mg, Protein: 10.6g

Tip: You can add a teaspoon of rosemary to the recipe to enhance the flavor of the bread.

114. Caramelized Onion Focaccia Bread

Prep Time: 5 minutes or less
Ready Time: 1 hours 10 minutes

12 Slices/1 ½ pounds
- 1 cup water
- 1 ½ teaspoon salt
- 3 cups bread flour
- 1 ½ tablespoons sugar
- 2 teaspoons yeast
- 3 ½ tablespoons butter
- 2 ½ minced garlic cloves
- 2 ½ tablespoons olive oil
- 2 sliced medium onions
- 1 cup shredded mozzarella cheese
- 2 ½ tablespoons shredded parmesan cheese

16 Slices/2 pounds
- 1 ½ cups water
- 1 ¾ teaspoons salt
- 4 cups bread flour
- 2 tablespoons sugar
- 2 ½ teaspoons yeast

- 4 tablespoons butter
- 3 minced garlic cloves
- 3 tablespoons olive oil
- 2 3 sliced medium onions
- 1 ½ cup shredded mozzarella cheese
- 3 tablespoons shredded parmesan cheese

Directions:

1. Place the ingredients except onion, garlic and cheese in the bread machine pan according to the manufacturer's recommended order.
2. Select the Dough Cycle on your bread machine, and Start.
3. Once the dough is done, take it out of the bread machine pan and place on a lightly floured surface.
4. Turn it into a 12" inch round into a greased cookie sheet.
5. Prepare the onion topping by cooking butter, garlic and onion in a pan over medium heat.
6. Remove from heat once the onions turn brown and become fragrant.
7. Make indentations in the dough with your fingertips and add the onion topping over it.
8. Cover with cheese and bake in a preheated oven for 15 to 20 minutes at 400 degrees F.
9. Take out the bread when done, cool slightly and slice to serve.

Nutrition:
Per Serving Calories: 479, Total Fat: 21.5g, Saturated Fat: 9.7g, Carbohydrates: 58g, Fiber: 2.8g, Sodium: 817mg, Protein: 13.3g

Tip: Serve the bread with olive oil for a rich flavor.

115. Olive Focaccia Bread

Prep Time: 5 minutes or less
Ready Time: 2 hours 10 minutes

12 Slices/1 ½ pounds
- ½ teaspoon salt
- 3 cups bread flour
- 2 tablespoons olive oil
- 1 cup water, lukewarm
- 2 tablespoons olive oil
- 2 teaspoons chopped garlic

- 1 ½ teaspoons active dry yeast
- 1 tablespoon chopped fresh rosemary
- 1 ½ teaspoons chopped fresh rosemary

16 Slices/2 pounds
- 1 teaspoon salt
- 4 cups bread flour
- 2 ½ tablespoons olive oil
- 1 ½ cup water, lukewarm
- 2 ½ tablespoons olive oil
- 2 ½ teaspoons chopped garlic
- 2 teaspoons active dry yeast
- 1 ½ tablespoon chopped fresh rosemary
- 2 teaspoons chopped fresh rosemary

Directions:

1. Place the ingredients except onion, garlic and cheese in the bread machine pan according to the manufacturer's recommended order.
2. Select the Dough Cycle on your bread machine, and Start.
3. Once the dough is done, take it out of the bread machine pan and place on a lightly floured surface.
4. Pat dough into a 12" pizza pan or 9x13 baking pan.
5. Make indentations in the dough with your fingertips and apply the remaining olive oil and rosemary over it.
6. Bake in a preheated oven at 400 degrees F for 20 to 30 minutes, or until golden-brown.
7. Take out the bread when done, cool slightly and slice to serve.

Nutrition:
Per Serving Calories: 156, Total Fat: 4.8g, Saturated Fat: 0.7g, Carbohydrates: 24.2g, Fiber: 1g, Sodium: 98.4mg, Protein: 3.5g

Tip: Serve the bread with a little olive oil, balsamic vinegar, and shredded cheese for the best tasting experience.

116. Onion & Herbs Focaccia

Prep Time: 5 minutes or less
Ready Time: 30 minutes

12 Slices/1 ½ pounds
- 1 cup warm water
- 1 tablespoon sugar
- 1 ½ teaspoons salt
- ¼ teaspoon salt, for topping
- ½ teaspoon pepper
- ⅛ teaspoon pepper, for topping
- 1 tablespoon olive oil
- ½ teaspoon dill weed
- 3 cups all-purpose flour
- ½ teaspoon dried basil
- ½ teaspoon garlic powder
- 2 teaspoons active dry yeast
- ⅓ cup onion, finely chopped
- ½ teaspoon dried parsley flakes
- 1 teaspoon grated parmesan cheese
- ½ teaspoon grated parmesan cheese, for topping

16 Slices/2 pounds
- 1 ½ cups warm water
- 1 ½ tablespoons sugar
- 1 ¾ teaspoons salt
- ½ teaspoon salt, for topping
- 1 teaspoon pepper
- ¼ teaspoon pepper, for topping
- 1 ½ tablespoons olive oil
- 1 teaspoon dill weed
- 4 cups all-purpose flour
- 1 teaspoon dried basil
- 1 teaspoon garlic powder
- 2 ½ teaspoons active dry yeast
- ½ cup onion, finely chopped
- 1 teaspoon dried parsley flakes
- 1 ½ teaspoon grated parmesan cheese
- 1 teaspoon grated parmesan cheese, for topping

Directions:
1. Add water, onion, sugar, salt, cheese, garlic, basil, dill, pepper, flour, yeast, parsley, and oil in the bread machine pan according to the manufacturer's recommended order.
2. Once dough is complete, put dough on a greased baking sheet and make indentations in it with your fingertips.
3. Pat it into a 9" round and sprinkle the top with the toppings.
4. Cover and allow to rise for 45 minutes in a warm place until it doubles in size.
5. Bake for 15 to 20 minutes or until golden-brown at 400 degrees.
6. Take out the bread when done, cool slightly and slice to serve.

Nutrition:
Per Serving Calories: 400, Total Fat: 4.7g, Saturated Fat: 0.8g, Carbohydrates: 77g, Fiber: 3.5g, Sodium: 1032mg, Protein: 11g

Tip: This bread is best served warm, so toast it before serving if you save it for the next day.

117. Focaccia Flat Bread

Prep Time: 5 minutes or less
Ready Time: 1 hour 45 minutes

12 Slices/1 ½ pounds
- 1 teaspoon salt
- 1 ½ cups water
- 1 tablespoon oil
- 3 cups bread flour
- 1 tablespoon sugar
- 2 teaspoons dried yeast
- 1 teaspoon dried rosemary
- 1 teaspoon dried oregano

16 Slices/2 pounds
- 1 ½ teaspoons salt
- 2 cups water
- 1 ½ tablespoons oil
- 4 cups bread flour
- 1 ½ tablespoons sugar
- 2 ½ teaspoons dried yeast
- 1 ½ teaspoons dried rosemary

- 1 ½ teaspoons dried oregano

Directions:
1. Place the ingredients in the bread machine pan according to the manufacturer's recommended order.
2. Select the Dough Cycle on your bread machine, and Start.
3. Once the dough is done, take it out of the bread machine pan and place on a lightly floured surface.
4. Gently knead it for 10 minutes and place in an oiled bowl.
5. Cover with a damp cloth and place in a warm location to rise for half an hour.
6. Knead the dough again in the bowl for a minute.
7. Turn it into a rectangular shape of 20x30 inches by using your hands.
8. Place the rectangle on your greased baking sheet and leave to rise again in a warm place for an hour.
9. Make indentations in the dough with your fingertips using a tablespoon of olive oil while doing so.
10. Top up with salt, basil, cheese, black olives, sun-dried tomatoes if you like to enhance the flavor further or omit and bake for 15 minutes at 225 degrees.

Nutrition:
Per Serving Calories: 130, Total Fat: 1.5g, Saturated Fat: 0.2g, Carbohydrates: 25.3g, Fiber: 1.1g, Sodium: 196mg, Protein: 3.5g

Tip: This recipe is versatile and you can be experimental with your toppings like mentioned in the directions.

Chapter 12: Sourdough Bread Recipes

118. Easy Sourdough Bread

Prep Time: 10 minutes or less
Ready Time: 1 - 2 hours

12 Slices/1 ½ pounds
- ¾ cup water
- 1 ½ teaspoon salt
- 3 cups bread flour
- ½ cup plain yogurt
- 1 tablespoon canola oil
- 1 tablespoon lemon juice
- 2 teaspoons active dry yeast

16 Slices/2 pounds
- 1 cup water
- 2 teaspoons salt
- 4 cups bread flour
- 1 cup plain yogurt
- 1 ½ tablespoon canola oil
- 1 ½ tablespoon lemon juice
- 2 ½ teaspoons active dry yeast

Directions:
1. Place the ingredients in the bread machine pan according to the manufacturer's recommended order.
2. Select the French Bread Cycle (if available) or White Bread setting on your bread machine, and press Start.
3. When the bread is done, take it out and let it cool on a cooling rack.
4. Slice and enjoy or store in an airtight container for a week.
5.

Nutrition:
Per Serving Calories: 134, Total Fat: 1.6g, Saturated Fat: 0g, Carbohydrates: 24g, Fiber: 1g, Sodium: 300mg, Protein: 4g

Tip: Simply add water instead of milk if you are want a softer bread.

119. Tangy Sourdough Bread

Prep Time: 10 minutes or less
Ready Time: 3 hours 15 minutes

12 Slices/1 ½ pounds
- 2 teaspoons salt
- 3 tablespoons oil
- 3 cups bread flour
- 1 tablespoon sugar
- ¾ cup warm water
- 1 cup sourdough starter
- 1 tablespoon active dry yeast

16 Slices/2 pounds
- 2 teaspoons salt
- 3 ½ tablespoons oil
- 4 cups bread flour
- 1 ½ tablespoon sugar
- 1 cup warm water
- 1 ¼ cup sourdough starter
- 1 ½ tablespoon active dry yeast

Directions:
1. Combine sourdough starter, water, sugar and yeast in a bowl and mix gently.
2. Put aside for 10 minutes until it starts bubbling.
3. Add this along with other ingredients to the bread machine pan.
4. Select the Basic setting with a light crust.
5. When the bread is done, take it out and let it cool on a cooling rack.
6. Slice and enjoy or store in an airtight container for a week.

Nutrition:
Per Serving Calories: 134, Total Fat: 1.6g, Saturated Fat: 0g, Carbohydrates: 24g, Fiber: 1g, Sodium: 300mg, Protein: 4g

Tip: Your sourdough starter should be active and bubbly before using in this recipe.

120. Bread Machine Sourdough

Prep Time: 10 minutes or less
Ready Time: 1 hour

12 Slices/1 ½ pounds

- ¾ cup water
- 3 cups flour
- 1 teaspoon salt
- 1 ½ teaspoons yeast
- 2 teaspoons margarine
- 2 teaspoons lemon juice
- ⅓ cup plain low-fat yogurt
- 1 tablespoon bread enhancer

16 Slices/2 pounds

- 1 cup water
- 4 cups flour
- 1 ½ teaspoons salt
- 2 teaspoons yeast
- 2 ½ teaspoons margarine
- 2 ½ teaspoons lemon juice
- ½ cup plain low-fat yogurt
- 1 ½ tablespoon bread enhancer

Directions:

1. Place all the ingredients in the bread machine pan according to the manufacturer's recommended order.
2. Select the Basic setting with a light crust.
3. When the bread is done, take it out and let it cool on a cooling rack.
4. Slice and enjoy or store in an airtight container for a week.

Nutrition:

Per Serving Calories: 1536, Total Fat: 12.4g, Saturated Fat: 2.5g, Carbohydrates: 305g, Fiber: 11.4g, Sodium: 2475mg, Protein: 44g

Tip: You can add a tablespoon of wheat germ for an even more delicious taste.

121. Rosemary Sourdough Bread

Prep Time: 10 minutes or less
Ready Time: 3 hours 10 minutes

12 Slices/1 ½ pounds

- ¾ cup water
- 1 ½ teaspoons salt
- 3 ½ cups bread flour
- 3 tablespoons sugar
- 1 teaspoon dried parsley
- 1 ¼ cups sourdough starter
- 2 tablespoons soy margarine
- 1 ½ teaspoons dried rosemary

16 Slices/2 pounds

- 1 cup water
- 1 ¾ teaspoons salt
- 4 ½ cups bread flour
- 3 ½ tablespoons sugar
- 1 ½ teaspoons dried parsley
- 1 ½ cups sourdough starter
- 2 ½ tablespoons soy margarine
- 2 teaspoons dried rosemary

Directions:

1. Place all the ingredients in the bread machine pan according to the manufacturer's recommended order.
2. Select the Basic setting with a Light crust.
3. Keep a check on the dough during the kneading cycle, add more flour if needed.
4. When the bread is done, take it out and let it cool on a cooling rack.
5. Slice and enjoy or store in an airtight container for a week.

Nutrition:

Per Serving Calories: 1719, Total Fat: 26g, Saturated Fat: 4.5g, Carbohydrates: 325g, Fiber: 10.9g, Sodium: 3805mg, Protein: 39g

Tip: You can substitute dried parsley with mixed Italian herbs or any herbs you like for personal preference.

122. Rye Sourdough Bread

Prep Time: 10 minutes or less
Ready Time: 3 hours 30 minutes

12 Slices/1 ½ pounds
- 1 large egg
- ⅓ cup water
- ¾ cup rye flour
- 2 tablespoons oil
- 1 ½ teaspoons salt
- 1 ½ teaspoons molasses
- 1 ½ tablespoons honey
- 1 cup sourdough starter
- 2 tablespoons caraway seeds
- 1 ½ teaspoons instant yeast
- 4 teaspoons vital wheat gluten
- 2 ¼ cups unbleached all-purpose flour

16 Slices/2 pounds
- 2 large eggs
- ½ cup water
- 1 cup rye flour
- 2 ½ tablespoons oil
- 1 ¾ teaspoons salt
- 2 teaspoons molasses
- 2 tablespoons honey
- 1 ½ cups sourdough starter
- 2 ½ tablespoons caraway seeds
- 2 teaspoons instant yeast
- 4 ½ teaspoons vital wheat gluten
- 3 ¼ cups unbleached all-purpose flour

Directions:
1. Place all the ingredients in the bread machine pan according to the manufacturer's recommended order.
2. Select the Dough Cycle and let it make the dough.
3. Keep an eye on the dough if it needs extra liquid or flour to adjust.
4. Bake by selecting the Basic setting with a Medium crust.
5. When the bread is done, take it out and let it cool on a cooling rack.
6. Slice and enjoy or store in an airtight container for a week.

Nutrition:
Per Serving Calories: 1791, Total Fat: 38g, Saturated Fat: 4.5g, Carbohydrates: 315g, Fiber: 23g, Sodium: 357mg, Protein: 39g

Tip: You can substitute salt with kosher or sea salt for personal preference.

123. Basic Sourdough Bread

Prep Time: 10 minutes or less
Ready Time: 3 hours 3 minutes

12 Slices/1 ½ pounds
- ¾ cup water
- 1 ½ teaspoons yeast
- 2 ⅔ cups bread flour
- 1 cup sourdough starter

16 Slices/2 pounds
- 1 cup water
- 2 teaspoons yeast
- 3 ⅔ cups bread flour
- 1 ½ cup sourdough starter

Directions:
1. Always follow the instructions on your sourdough starter of using it before baking a bread.
2. Place all the ingredients in the bread machine pan according to the manufacturer's recommended order.
3. Bake by selecting the Basic setting with a Medium crust.
4. When the bread is done, take it out and let it cool on a cooling rack.
5. Slice and enjoy or store in an airtight container for a week.

Nutrition:
Per Serving Calories: 822, Total Fat: 2.5g, Saturated Fat: 0g, Carbohydrates: 171g, Fiber: 71g, Sodium: 2335mg, Protein: 24g

Tip: Instead of using bread flour, you can try a combination of 2 cups white flour, ⅓ cups wheat bran and ⅓ cups flaxseed meal. This combination works perfectly well if you like a multigrain sourdough.

124. Sourdough Bread with A Twist

Prep Time: 5 minutes or less
Ready Time: 3 hours 5 minutes

12 Slices/1 ½ pounds
- ¾ cup water
- 2 ½ bread flour
- ½ cup barley flour
- 1 ⅛ teaspoons salt
- 1 tablespoon vegetable oil
- 2 tablespoons white sugar
- 2 tablespoons dry potato flakes
- 1 ½ teaspoons active dry yeast
- ¾ cup sour cream, room temperature

16 Slices/2 pounds
- 1 cup water
- 3 ½ bread flour
- ½ cup barley flour
- 1 ¼ teaspoons salt
- 1 ½ tablespoons vegetable oil
- 2 ½ tablespoons white sugar
- 2 ½ tablespoons dry potato flakes
- 2 ½ teaspoons active dry yeast
- 1 cup sour cream, room temperature

Directions:
1. Place all the ingredients in the bread machine pan according to the manufacturer's recommended order.
2. Select the White Bread setting with light crust and preferable loaf size.
3. When the bread is done, take it out and let it cool on a cooling rack.
4. Slice and enjoy or store in an airtight container for a week.

Nutrition:
Per Serving Calories: 2017, Total Fat: 54g, Saturated Fat: 25g, Carbohydrates: 333g, Fiber: 17g, Sodium: 2729mg, Protein: 48g

Tip: To add a nice texture to the bread, grind some barley groats and add them to the recipe.

125. Multigrain Sourdough Bread

Prep Time: 5 minutes or less
Ready Time: 50 minutes

12 Slices/1 ½ pounds
- ¼ cup sugar
- 1 ½ teaspoons salt
- ¼ cup potato flakes
- 4 tablespoons butter
- ⅓ cup rolled oatmeal
- 1 cup evaporated milk
- ¼ cup rolled wheat flakes
- 1 ⅓ cups proofed sourdough starter
- 2 tablespoons whole ground flaxseed meal
- 3 ½ cups plus 2 tablespoons white bread flour

16 Slices/2 pounds
- ½ cup sugar
- 1 ¾ teaspoons salt
- ½ cup potato flakes
- 4 ½ tablespoons butter
- ½ cup rolled oatmeal
- 1 ½ cup evaporated milk
- ½ cup rolled wheat flakes
- 1 ½ cups proofed sourdough starter
- 2 ½ tablespoons whole ground flaxseed meal
- 4 ½ cups plus 2 tablespoons white bread flour

Directions:
1. Place all the ingredients in the bread machine pan according to the manufacturer's recommended order.
2. Select the Dough Cycle and let the machine do its thing.
3. Once the kneading cycle ends, take out the dough without letting it rise.
4. You might need to use an oil spray to carefully remove the dough as it might be soft.
5. Shape the dough into your preferred shape and let it rise in a greased loaf pan until it doubles in size, usually it takes 3-4 hours.
6. Bake for 30 minutes in the oven at 350 degrees.
7. Remove the bread from the pan once done and baste the top with butter.

8. Put it on a cooling rack and slice after 25 minutes.

Nutrition:
Per Serving Calories: 2623, Total Fat: 77g, Saturated Fat: 42g, Carbohydrates: 415g, Fiber: 19g, Sodium: 4163mg, Protein: 67g

Tip: If you are using a stoneware loaf pan, make sure to grease it with oil and cover the sides and bottom with cornmeal.

126. Overnight Sourdough Bread

Prep Time: 5 minutes or less
Ready Time: 14 hours 2 minutes

12 Slices/1 ½ pounds
- ½ cup water
- ¼ teaspoon salt
- ½ cup bread flour, for overnight starter
- 6 ½ tablespoons milk
- ½ teaspoon vinegar
- 2 ½ cups bread flour
- ½ teaspoon white sugar
- ⅛ teaspoon white sugar, for overnight starter
- ½ tablespoon vegetable oil
- 1 ½ teaspoons active dry yeast
- 1 ½ teaspoons active dry yeast, for overnight starter

16 Slices/2 pounds
- 1 cup water
- ½ teaspoon salt
- 1 cup bread flour, for overnight starter
- 7 tablespoons milk
- 1 teaspoon vinegar
- 3 cups bread flour
- 1 teaspoon white sugar
- ¼ teaspoon white sugar, for overnight starter
- 1 tablespoon vegetable oil
- 2 teaspoons active dry yeast
- 2 teaspoons active dry yeast, for overnight starter

Directions:
1. Combine the overnight starter ingredients: bread flour, sugar, water, and yeast in a bowl and mix thoroughly.
2. Seal with plastic and leave in a warm location for 6 to 8 hours, or overnight.
3. Pour the mixture, the next day, into the bread machine pan with the remaining ingredients as ordered by the manufacturer.
4. Select the appropriate cycle and Start.
5. When the bread is done, take it out and let it cool on a cooling rack.
6. Slice and enjoy or store in an airtight container for a week.

Nutrition:
Per Serving Calories: 208, Total Fat: 2.4g, Saturated Fat: 0.5g, Carbohydrates: 39.8g, Fiber: 1.8g, Sodium: 124mg, Protein: 6.2g

Tip: You can use a combination of all-purpose and bread flour if you are short on the latter.

127. Czech Sourdough Bread

Prep Time: 5 minutes or less
Ready Time: 24 hours 15 minutes

12 Slices/1 ½ pounds
- 1 tablespoon salt
- 1 cup bread flour
- 1 ½ cups rye flour
- ¾ cup wheat flour
- 1 tablespoon honey
- 1 cup non-dairy milk
- 1 cup sourdough starter
- 2 teaspoons caraway seeds
- 5 tablespoons wheat gluten
- ½ cup grated half-baked potato

16 Slices/2 pounds
- 1 ½ tablespoons salt
- 1 ½ cups bread flour
- 1 ¾ cups rye flour
- 1 cup wheat flour
- 1 ½ tablespoons honey
- 1 ½ cups non-dairy milk
- 1 ½ cup sourdough starter

- 2 ½ teaspoons caraway seeds
- 5 ½ tablespoons wheat gluten
- 1 cup grated half-baked potato

Directions:
1. Place all the ingredients in the bread machine pan according to the manufacturer's recommended order.
2. Select the Dough Cycle and let the machine do its thing.
3. The dough will take 24 hours to double in size in the bread machine.
4. Bake it once it does in the bread machine for an hour with appropriate cycle and loaf size.
5. Take it out to cool on a cooling rack before removing from pan.
6. Slice and enjoy!

Nutrition:
Per Serving Calories: 198, Total Fat: 1.9g, Saturated Fat: 0.8g, Carbohydrates: 39.9g, Fiber: 4.3g, Sodium: 888mg, Protein: 6.5g

Tip: You can substitute non-dairy milk with whole milk if you are not lactose-intolerant.

128. Amish Sourdough Bread

Prep Time: 5 minutes or less
Ready Time: 3 hours 35 minutes

12 Slices/1 ½ pounds
- ½ tablespoon oil
- 1 ½ teaspoons salt
- 3 cups bread flour
- ½ cup hot tap water
- ½ cup amish starter
- 1 ½ teaspoons active dry yeast

16 Slices/2 pounds
- 1 tablespoon oil
- 2 teaspoons salt
- 4 cups bread flour
- 1 cup hot tap water
- 1 cup amish starter
- 2 teaspoons active dry yeast

Directions:
1. Place all the ingredients in the bread machine pan according to the manufacturer's recommended order.
2. Select the French Bread setting with Light Crust.
3. When the bread is done, take it out and let it cool on a cooling rack.
4. Slice and enjoy or store in an airtight container for a week.

Nutrition:
Per Serving Calories: 196, Total Fat: 1.9g, Saturated Fat: 0.3g, Carbohydrates: 38.5g, Fiber: 1.6g, Sodium: 467mg, Protein: 5.5g

Tip: Serve this bread with cheese or make a grilled chicken sandwich for the best experience.

129. Sourdough Bread with Beer

Prep Time: 5 minutes or less
Ready Time: 3 hours 5 minutes

12 Slices/1 ½ pounds
- ¼ cup water
- ½ cup flat beer
- 3 cups bread flour
- 1 ½ teaspoons salt
- 1 tablespoon sugar
- 1 ½ teaspoons yeast
- 2 tablespoons vegetable oil
- 1 ⅓ cups sourdough starter

16 Slices/2 pounds
- ½ cup water
- 1 cup flat beer
- 4 cups bread flour
- 1 ¾ teaspoons salt
- 1 ½ tablespoon sugar
- 2 teaspoons yeast
- 2 ½ tablespoons vegetable oil
- 1 ½ cups sourdough starter

Directions:
1. Place all the ingredients in the bread machine pan according to the manufacturer's recommended order.

2. Select the White Bread setting with Dark Crust, and Start.
3. When the bread is done, take it out and let it cool on a cooling rack.
4. Slice and enjoy or store in an airtight container for a week.

Nutrition:
Per Serving Calories: 143, Total Fat: 2.6g, Saturated Fat: 0.3g, Carbohydrates: 25.4g, Fiber: 0.9g, Sodium: 292mg, Protein: 3.5g

Tip: If you don't know how to flatten beer, pour it in a saucepan and bring to a simmer on medium heat. Turn off heat and as the beer starts to cool down, it will become flat.

130. Sourdough Bread with Oatmeal

Prep Time: 10 minutes or less
Ready Time: 3 hours 10 minutes

12 Slices/1 ½ pounds
- 1 ¼ teaspoons salt
- 1 cup oatmeal
- 1 ½ teaspoons yeast
- 1 ½ tablespoons olive oil
- 1 ¾ cups sourdough starter
- 2 ½ tablespoons milk or buttermilk
- 1 ½ tablespoon honey or maple syrup
- 2 cups bread flour or all-purpose unbleached flour

16 Slices/2 pounds
- 1 ½ teaspoons salt
- 1 ¾ cup oatmeal
- 2 teaspoons yeast
- 2 tablespoons olive oil
- 1 ¾ cups sourdough starter
- 3 tablespoons milk or buttermilk
- 2 tablespoon honey or maple syrup
- 2 ½ cups bread flour or all-purpose unbleached flour

Directions:
1. Place all the ingredients in the bread machine pan according to the manufacturer's recommended order.
2. Select the Dough Cycle and let the machine do its thing.
3. Take out the dough once done and shape into a loaf.
4. Cover to let it rise until it doubles in size, for 40 minutes to an hour.
5. Next, bake in the oven for 40 minutes at 350 degrees.
6. When the bread is done, take it out and let it cool on a cooling rack.
7. Slice and enjoy or store in an airtight container for a week.

Nutrition:
Per Serving Calories: 173, Total Fat: 3.2g, Saturated Fat: 0.6g, Carbohydrates: 31.5g, Fiber: 1.5g, Sodium: 391mg, Protein: 4.3g

Tip: If you are using a starter and zero yeast, leave the dough to rise overnight. This will give the dough plenty of time to rise beautifully.

Chapter 13: Holiday Bread Recipes

131. Pure Whole Wheat Bread

Prep Time: 5 minutes or less
Ready Time: 4 hours 20 minutes

12 Slices/1 ½ pounds
- 2 cups warm water
- 1 teaspoon salt
- 3 whole wheat flour
- 1 ½ tablespoons butter
- 1 ½ tablespoons honey
- 1 ½ tablespoons olive oil
- 1 ½ tablespoons vital wheat gluten
- 1 ½ teaspoons bread machine yeast

16 Slices/2 pounds
- 3 cups warm water
- 1 ½ teaspoons salt
- 4 whole wheat flour
- 2 tablespoons butter
- 2 tablespoons honey
- 2 tablespoons olive oil
- 2 tablespoons vital wheat gluten
- 1 ¾ teaspoons bread machine yeast

Directions:
1. Place ingredients in the bread machine pan according to the manufacturer's recommended order.
2. Select the Whole Wheat cycle with preferable crust and loaf size on your bread machine, and press Start.
3. When the bread is done, unplug the machine and remove the pan.
4. Gently shake the bucket to remove the bread, and place it on a cooling rack.
5. Slice after 10 minutes and enjoy!

Nutrition:
Per Serving Calories: 186, Total Fat: 4g, Saturated Fat: 1g, Carbohydrates: 33g, Fiber: 5g, Sodium: 242mg, Protein: 6g

Tip: Use water according to the flour weight. Keep an eye on the dough, if it's too stiff, you can add more water.

132. Carrot & Thyme Yeast Bread

Prep Time: 5 minutes or less
Ready Time: 3 hours 5 minutes

12 Slices/1 ½ pounds
- 1 cup water
- 1 cup rye flour
- ½ cup cornmeal
- 1 ½ teaspoons salt
- 2 ¾ cups bread flour
- 2 cups grated carrots
- 3 tablespoons vegetable oil
- 1 ½ tablespoons white sugar
- 1 ½ tablespoons dried thyme
- 2 ½ teaspoons active dry yeast

16 Slices/2 pounds
- 1 ½ cups water
- 1 ½ cups rye flour
- 1 cup cornmeal
- 1 ¾ teaspoons salt
- 3 ¼ cups bread flour
- 2 ½ cups grated carrots
- 3 ½ tablespoons vegetable oil
- 2 tablespoons white sugar
- 2 tablespoons dried thyme
- 2 ¾ teaspoons active dry yeast

Directions:
1. Place ingredients in the bread machine pan according to the manufacturer's recommended order.
2. Select the Basic Bread cycle with preferable crust and loaf size on your bread machine, and press Start.
3. When the bread is done, unplug the machine and remove the pan.
4. Gently shake the bucket to remove the bread, and place it on a cooling rack.
5. Slice after 10 minutes and enjoy!

Nutrition:

Per Serving Calories: 190, Total Fat: 4g, Saturated Fat: 1g, Carbohydrates: 33g, Fiber: 3g, Sodium: 307mg, Protein: 5g

Tip: If you want a stronger flavor, increase the quantity of salt. Also, you can substitute white sugar with honey in case of availability issues.

133. Oatmeal & Honey Multigrain Bread

Prep Time: 5 minutes or less
Ready Time: 3 hours 5 minutes

12 Slices/1 ½ pounds
- 1 cup milk
- 1 cup water
- 1 ¼ teaspoons salt
- 2 cups bread flour
- ½ cup rolled oats
- ¼ cup wheat germ
- 1 ½ tablespoons butter
- 2 ½ tablespoons honey
- 2 ¼ cups whole wheat flour
- 2 ½ teaspoons active dry yeast

16 Slices/1 ½ pounds
- 1 ½ cups milk
- 1 ½ cups water
- 1 ½ teaspoons salt
- 3 cups bread flour
- 1 cup rolled oats
- ½ cup wheat germ
- 2 tablespoons butter
- 3 tablespoons honey
- 2 ½ cups whole wheat flour
- 2 ¾ teaspoons active dry yeast

Directions:
1. Place ingredients in the bread machine pan according to the manufacturer's recommended order.
2. Select the Multigrain cycle with preferable crust and loaf size on your bread machine, and press Start.
3. When the bread is done, unplug the machine and remove the pan.
4. Gently shake the bucket to remove the bread, and place it on a cooling rack.

5. Slice after 10 minutes and enjoy!

Nutrition:
Per Serving Calories: 147, Total Fat: 2g, Saturated Fat: 1g, Carbohydrates: 28g, Fiber: 3g, Sodium: 251mg, Protein: 5g

Tip: For a fluffier bread, add a tablespoon of vital gluten wheat and flax meal.

134. Moist Peanut Butter Bread

Prep Time: 5 minutes or less
Ready Time: 3 hours 5 minutes

12 Slices/1 ½ pounds
- 1 egg
- 1 teaspoon salt
- 3 cups bread flour
- 1 cup warm water
- 2 tablespoons honey
- 1 tablespoon white sugar
- 1 tablespoon brown sugar
- 1 tablespoon vegetable oil
- 1 ½ teaspoons active dry yeast
- 3 tablespoons crunchy or creamy peanut butter

16 Slices/2 pounds
- 2 eggs
- 1 ½ teaspoons salt
- 4 cups bread flour
- 1 ½ cups warm water
- 2 ½ tablespoons honey
- 1 ½ tablespoons white sugar
- 1 ½ tablespoons brown sugar
- 1 ½ tablespoons vegetable oil
- 2 teaspoons active dry yeast
- 3 ½ tablespoons crunchy or creamy peanut butter

Directions:
1. Place ingredients in the bread machine pan according to the manufacturer's recommended order.
2. Select the White Bread cycle with preferable crust and loaf size on your bread machine, and press Start.

3. When the bread is done, unplug the machine and remove the pan.
4. Gently shake the bucket to remove the bread, and place it on a cooling rack.
5. Slice after 10 minutes and enjoy!

Nutrition:
Per Serving Calories: 184, Total Fat: 4g, Saturated Fat: 1g, Carbohydrates: 31g, Fiber: 1g, Sodium: 221mg, Protein: 6g

Tip: Serve this bread with extra peanut butter or jam for an enjoyable experience.

135. Cereal Grain Bread

Prep Time: 5 minutes or less
Ready Time: 3 hours 5 minutes

12 Slices/1 ½ pounds
- 1 ¾ teaspoons salt
- 3 ¼ cups bread flour
- 1 ½ cups warm water
- 1 cup seven grain cereal
- 2 ½ tablespoons white sugar
- 2 tablespoons margarine
- 2 teaspoons active dry yeast
- 2 tablespoons nonfat dry milk powder

16 Slices/2 pounds
- 2 teaspoons salt
- 4 ¼ cups bread flour
- 1 ⅞ cups warm water
- 1 ½ cups seven grain cereal
- 3 tablespoons white sugar
- 2 ½ tablespoons margarine
- 2 ¼ teaspoons active dry yeast
- 2 ½ tablespoons nonfat dry milk powder

Directions:
1. Place ingredients in the bread machine pan according to the manufacturer's recommended order.
2. Select the Medium Dark Crust setting with loaf size on your bread machine, and press Start.
3. When the bread is done, unplug the machine and remove the pan.

4. Gently shake the bucket to remove the bread, and place it on a cooling rack.
5. Slice after 10 minutes and enjoy!

Nutrition:
Per Serving Calories: 142, Total Fat: 2g, Saturated Fat: 0g, Carbohydrates: 26g, Fiber: 2g, Sodium: 312mg, Protein: 5g

Tip: You can substitute bread flour with whole wheat flour and water with milk in case of availability issues.

136. Chocolate & Cinnamon Bread

Prep Time: 5 minutes or less
Ready Time: 3 hours 50 minutes

12 Slices/1 ½ pounds
- 1 egg
- 1 cup milk
- ¼ cup water
- 1 teaspoon salt
- 3 ⅓ cups bread flour
- 1 teaspoon cocoa powder
- 1 tablespoon vanilla extract
- ½ cup peanut butter chips
- 1 teaspoon ground cinnamon
- 1 ½ teaspoons active dry yeast
- ¼ cup semisweet chocolate chips
- 2 tablespoons margarine, softened
- ½ cup sucralose and brown sugar blend

16 Slices/2 pounds
- 2 eggs
- 1 ½ cup milk
- ½ cup water
- 1 ½ teaspoons salt
- 4 ⅓ cups bread flour
- 1 ½ teaspoons cocoa powder
- 1 ½ tablespoons vanilla extract
- 1 cup peanut butter chips
- 1 ½ teaspoon ground cinnamon
- 2 teaspoons active dry yeast
- ½ cup semisweet chocolate chips
- 2 ½ tablespoons margarine, softened
- 1 cup sucralose and brown sugar blend

Directions:

1. Place ingredients except chocolate and peanut butter chips in the bread machine pan according to the manufacturer's recommended order.
2. Add the chips 10 minutes before the kneading cycle ends, or when the machine beeps for add-in ingredients.
3. Select the Light Crust setting with loaf size on your bread machine, and press Start.
4. When the bread is done, unplug the machine and remove the pan.
5. Gently shake the bucket to remove the bread, and place it on a cooling rack.
6. Slice after 10 minutes and enjoy!

Nutrition:

Per Serving Calories: 122, Total Fat: 7g, Saturated Fat: 4g, Carbohydrates: 11g, Fiber: 1g, Sodium: 259mg, Protein: 4g

Tip: Add more flour if the dough is wet to make it soft and pliable.

137. Golden Syrup Bread

Prep Time: 5 minutes or less
Ready Time: 3 hours 5 minutes

12 Slices/1 ½ pounds

- 3 cups bread flour
- 1 ½ teaspoons salt
- ½ cup golden raisins
- 1 ¼ cups warm water
- 1 tablespoon bread flour
- 2 tablespoons vegetable oil
- 1 tablespoon active dry yeast
- 1 teaspoon ground cinnamon
- 1 ½ tablespoons golden syrup
- 2 tablespoons instant powdered milk

16 Slices/2 pounds

- 4 cups bread flour
- 1 ¾ teaspoons salt
- ¾ cup golden raisins
- 1 ½ cups warm water
- 1 ½ tablespoons bread flour
- 2 ½ tablespoons vegetable oil

- 1 ½ tablespoons active dry yeast
- 1 ½ teaspoons ground cinnamon
- 2 tablespoons golden syrup
- 2 ½ tablespoons instant powdered milk

Directions:

1. Place ingredients in the bread machine pan according to the manufacturer's recommended order.
2. Select the White Bread setting with loaf size on your bread machine, and press Start.
3. When the bread is done, unplug the machine and remove the pan.
4. Gently shake the bucket to remove the bread, and place it on a cooling rack.
5. Slice after 10 minutes and enjoy!

Nutrition:

Per Serving Calories: 356, Total Fat: 6g, Saturated Fat: 1g, Carbohydrates: 66g, Fiber: 3g, Sodium: 597mg, Protein: 11g

Tip: You can substitute golden syrup with light corn syrup in case of availability issues.

138. Zucchini Whole Wheat Bread

Prep Time: 5 minutes or less
Ready Time: 3 hours 5 minutes

12 Slices/1 ½ pounds

- 1 cup water
- 1 ¼ teaspoons salt
- 2 ½ teaspoons honey
- 2 ½ cups bread flour
- 1 cup grated zucchini
- 1 cup whole wheat flour
- 2 ½ teaspoons sesame seeds
- 1 ½ tablespoons vegetable oil
- 1 ¾ teaspoons active dry yeast
- 1 ½ tablespoon chopped fresh basil

16 Slices/2 pounds

- 1 ½ cups water
- 1 ½ teaspoons salt
- 3 teaspoons honey
- 3 cups bread flour
- 1 ½ cups grated zucchini

- 1 ½ cup whole wheat flour
- 3 teaspoons sesame seeds
- 2 tablespoons vegetable oil
- 2 teaspoons active dry yeast
- 2 tablespoons chopped fresh basil

Directions:

1. Place ingredients in the bread machine pan according to the manufacturer's recommended order.
2. Select the Basic Bread, or Normal setting with loaf size on your bread machine, and press Start.
3. When the bread is done, unplug the machine and remove the pan.
4. Gently shake the bucket to remove the bread, and place it on a cooling rack.
5. Slice after 10 minutes and enjoy!

Nutrition:

Per Serving Calories: 153, Total Fat: 2g, Saturated Fat: 0g, Carbohydrates: 28g, Fiber: 2g, Sodium: 235mg, Protein: 5g

Tip: Sprinkle extra sesame seeds on top for a tastier, crunchier experience.

139. Christmas Limpa Bread

Prep Time: 5 minutes or less
Ready Time: 3 hours 5 minutes

12 Slices/1 ½ pounds

- 1 ½ cups rye flour
- 1 ½ cups bread flour
- ¼ cup cracked wheat
- 1 ⅓ cups boiling water
- 1 teaspoon fennel seed
- 2 ¼ tablespoons butter
- 1 teaspoon cumin seeds
- 1 teaspoon caraway seed
- 1 tablespoon orange zest
- ¼ teaspoon baking soda
- 2 teaspoons gluten flour
- 2 ¼ tablespoons molasses
- 2 teaspoons active dry yeast
- 3 tablespoons powdered buttermilk

16 Slices/2 pounds

- 2 cups rye flour
- 2 cups bread flour
- ½ cup cracked wheat
- 1 ¾ cups boiling water
- 1 ½ teaspoons fennel seed
- 2 ½ tablespoons butter
- 1 ½ teaspoons cumin seeds
- 1 ½ teaspoons caraway seed
- 1 ½ tablespoons orange zest
- ½ teaspoons baking soda
- 2 ½ teaspoons gluten flour
- 2 ½ tablespoons molasses
- 2 ½ teaspoons active dry yeast
- 3 ½ tablespoons powdered buttermilk

Directions:

1. Add all the seeds, butter, cracked wheat, molasses, and orange zest in 1 ⅓ cup boiling water and put aside to soak for an hour.
2. Next, add it along with the other ingredients to the bread machine pan in the manufacturer's recommended order.
3. Select the White Bread cycle with a light crust on your bread machine, and press Start.
4. When the bread is done, unplug the machine and remove the pan.
5. Gently shake the bucket to remove the bread, and place it on a cooling rack.
6. Slice after 10 minutes and enjoy!

Nutrition:

Per Serving Calories: 78, Total Fat: 2g, Saturated Fat: 1g, Carbohydrates: 13g, Fiber: 2g, Sodium: 42mg, Protein: 2g

Tip: You can substitute rye flour with whole wheat in case of availability issues.

140. Special Panettone Bread

Prep Time: 5 minutes or less
Ready Time: 3 hours 5 minutes

12 Slices/1 ½ pounds
- 2 eggs
- ¼ cup butter
- 1 ½ teaspoons salt
- ¾ cup warm water
- 3 ¼ cups bread flour
- 2 tablespoons white sugar
- 1 ½ teaspoons vanilla extract
- 2 tablespoons dry milk powder
- 2 teaspoons bread machine yeast
- ½ cup chopped dried mixed fruit

16 Slices/2 pounds
- 3 eggs
- ½ cup butter
- 1 ¾ teaspoons salt
- 1 cup warm water
- 4 ¼ cups bread flour
- 2 ½ tablespoons white sugar
- 2 teaspoons vanilla extract
- 2 ½ tablespoons dry milk powder
- 2 ½ teaspoons bread machine yeast
- 1 cup chopped dried mixed fruit

Directions:
1. Place ingredients except mixed fruit in the bread machine pan according to the manufacturer's recommended order.
2. Select the Sweet Bread, or Basic setting with preferable loaf size on your bread machine, and press Start.
3. Add the mixed fruit 5 to 10 minutes before the kneading cycle ends, or when the machine beeps for mix-in ingredients.
4. When the bread is done, unplug the machine and remove the pan.
5. Gently shake the bucket to remove the bread, and place it on a cooling rack.
6. Slice after 10 minutes and enjoy!

Nutrition:

Per Serving Calories: 93, Total Fat: 6g, Saturated Fat: 3g, Carbohydrates: 9g, Fiber: 2g, Sodium: 405mg, Protein: 2g

Tip: You can substitute bread machine yeast with instant or active dry yeast and butter with margarine in case of availability issues.

141. Easy Molasses Loaf Bread

Prep Time: 5 minutes or less
Ready Time: 3 hours 5 minutes

12 Slices/1 ½ pounds
- ¼ cup molasses
- 1 ½ teaspoons salt
- 1 ¾ cups water
- 3 cups bread flour
- 1 ½ tablespoons butter
- ½ tablespoon active dry yeast
- 1 ½ tablespoons dry milk powder

16 Slices/2 pounds
- ⅓ cup molasses
- 2 teaspoons salt
- 1 ⅝ cups water
- 4 cups bread flour
- 2 tablespoons butter
- 1 tablespoon active dry yeast
- 2 tablespoons dry milk powder

Directions:
1. Place ingredients in the bread machine pan according to the manufacturer's recommended order.
2. Select the White Bread, Light crust setting with preferable loaf size on your bread machine, and press Start.
3. When the bread is done, unplug the machine and remove the pan.
4. Gently shake the bucket to remove the bread, and place it on a cooling rack.
5. Slice after 10 minutes and enjoy!

Nutrition:
Per Serving Calories: 234, Total Fat: 3g, Saturated Fat: 2g, Carbohydrates: 44g, Fiber: 1g, Sodium: 420mg, Protein: 7g

Tip: You can substitute molasses with honey in case of availability issues.

142. Cheesy Rosemary Bread

Prep Time: 5 minutes or less
Ready Time: 3 hours 5 minutes

12 Slices/1 ½ pounds

- 1 cup oat bran
- 1 ½ teaspoons salt
- 2 ½ tablespoons honey
- 3 cups bread flour
- 1 ½ teaspoons garlic salt
- 1 ½ cups warm water
- ½ cup vital wheat gluten
- 1 cup whole wheat flour
- 1 cup grated Parmesan cheese
- 1 ½ teaspoons ground black pepper
- 2 ½ tablespoons extra virgin olive oil
- 1 cup shredded mozzarella cheese
- 2 ½ tablespoons chopped fresh rosemary
- 2 ½ teaspoons package active dry yeast

16 Slices/2 pounds

- 1 ½ cups oat bran
- 1 ¾ teaspoons salt
- 3 tablespoons honey
- 3 ½ cups bread flour
- 1 ¾ teaspoons garlic salt
- 1 ¾ cups warm water
- 1 cup vital wheat gluten
- 1 ½ cups whole wheat flour
- 1 ½ cups grated Parmesan cheese
- 1 ¾ teaspoons ground black pepper
- 3 tablespoons extra virgin olive oil
- 1 ½ cups shredded mozzarella cheese
- 3 tablespoons chopped fresh rosemary
- 2 ¾ teaspoons package active dry yeast

Directions:

1. Place ingredients in the bread machine pan according to the manufacturer's recommended order.
2. Select the Oat/French setting (if available) or White Bread cycle with preferable loaf size on your bread machine, and press Start.

3. When the bread is done, unplug the machine and remove the pan.
4. Gently shake the bucket to remove the bread, and place it on a cooling rack.
5. Slice after 10 minutes and enjoy!

Nutrition:

Per Serving Calories: 111, Total Fat: 5g, Saturated Fat: 2g, Carbohydrates: 14g, Fiber: 2g, Sodium: 426mg, Protein: 6g

Tip: Serve this bread with soup or eat with extra cheese for the best experience.

143. Persimmon Pulp Bread

Prep Time: 5 minutes or less
Ready Time: 3 hours 5 minutes

12 Slices/1 ½ pounds

- ⅓ cup raisins
- 2 cups bread flour
- 1 ½ teaspoons salt
- 9 tablespoons water
- 2 tablespoons butter
- 1 cup whole wheat flour
- 2 tablespoons wheat germ
- 1 ½ teaspoons white sugar
- 1 teaspoon ground cinnamon
- 2 ½ teaspoons active dry yeast
- ½ cup very ripe persimmon pulp

16 Slices/2 pounds

- ½ cup raisins
- 2 ½ cups bread flour
- 1 ¾ teaspoons salt
- 9 ½ tablespoons water
- 2 ½ tablespoons butter
- 1 ½ cup whole wheat flour
- 2 ½ tablespoons wheat germ
- 2 teaspoons white sugar
- 1 ½ teaspoon ground cinnamon
- 2 ¾ teaspoons active dry yeast
- ¾ cup very ripe persimmon pulp

Directions:

1. Place ingredients except raisins in the bread machine pan according to the manufacturer's recommended order.
2. Select the Basic/White setting with preferable loaf size on your bread machine, and press Start.
3. Add the raisins when the machine beeps for fruits/nuts, or 10 minutes before the kneading cycle ends.
4. When the bread is done, unplug the machine and remove the pan.
5. Gently shake the bucket to remove the bread, and place it on a cooling rack.
6. Slice after 10 minutes and enjoy!

Nutrition:
Per Serving Calories: 165, Total Fat: 3g, Saturated Fat: 1g, Carbohydrates: 31g, Fiber: 2g, Sodium: 307mg, Protein: 5g

Tip: Use more water if needed during the kneading cycle to make the dough soft.

144. Quick Banana Nut Bread

Prep Time: 5 minutes or less
Ready Time: 3 hours 5 minutes

12 Slices/1 ½ pounds
- 2 eggs
- ¾ cup milk
- 1 ¼ teaspoon salt
- 1 ½ cups white sugar
- ¾ cup mashed bananas
- ⅔ cup chopped walnuts
- ¾ teaspoon baking soda
- 3 ½ cups all-purpose flour
- ¾ cup margarine, softened
- 2 ¾ teaspoons baking powder

16 Slices/2 pounds
- 3 eggs
- 1 cup milk
- 1 ½ teaspoons salt
- 1 ¾ cups white sugar
- 1 cup mashed bananas
- ¾ cup chopped walnuts
- 1 teaspoon baking soda

- 4 ½ cups all-purpose flour
- 1 cup margarine, softened
- 3 teaspoons baking powder

Directions:
1. Place ingredients in the bread machine pan according to the manufacturer's recommended order.
2. Select the Quick/Cake setting with preferable loaf size on your bread machine, and press Start.
3. Check the bread to see if it's well-mixed, give a mix yourself.
4. When the bread is done, unplug the machine and remove the pan.
5. Gently shake the bucket to remove the bread, and place it on a cooling rack.
6. Slice after 10 minutes and enjoy!

Nutrition:
Per Serving Calories: 347, Total Fat: 15g, Saturated Fat: 3g, Carbohydrates: 49g, Fiber: 2g, Sodium: 561mg, Protein: 6g

Tip: We would recommend premixing the ingredients together before transferring them to the bread machine pan, so that everything is properly mixed.

145 Healthy Einkorn Bread Loaf

Prep Time: 5 minutes or less
Ready Time: 1 hour 55 minutes

12 Slices/1 ½ pounds
- ¼ cup milk
- 1 cup water
- ¼ cup oat flour
- ⅛ cup flax seeds
- 1 ½ cups spelt flour
- 1 teaspoon salt
- 1 ½ tablespoons butter
- 1 ½ cups einkorn flour
- 1 ½ tablespoons white sugar
- 1 ½ teaspoons fast-rising yeast

16 Slices/2 pounds
- ⅓ cup milk
- 1 ⅓ cups water

- ½ cup oat flour
- ¼ cup flax seeds
- 2 cups spelt flour
- 1 ½ teaspoons salt
- 2 tablespoons butter
- 2 cups einkorn flour
- 2 tablespoons white sugar
- 2 teaspoons fast-rising yeast

Directions:
1. Place ingredients in the bread machine pan according to the manufacturer's recommended order.
2. Select the Wheat setting with preferable loaf size on your bread machine, and press Start.
3. Check the bread to see if the dough is smooth, if not, add milk to get it right.
4. When the bread is done, unplug the machine and remove the pan.
5. Gently shake the bucket to remove the bread, and place it on a cooling rack.
6. Slice after 10 minutes and enjoy!

Nutrition:
Per Serving Calories: 118, Total Fat: 15g, Saturated Fat: 1g, Carbohydrates: 20g, Fiber: 2g, Sodium: 186mg, Protein: 4g

Tip: You can substitute einkorn or spelt with whole wheat and oat bran with oat flour in case of availability issues. If you choose to ditch einkorn flour for another substitute, you will need 20% less milk for the dough.

146. Almond High Protein Bread

Prep Time: 5 minutes or less
Ready Time: 3 hour 10 minutes

12 Slices/1 ½ pounds
- ¼ cup honey
- 1 ¼ cups water
- 1 teaspoon salt
- 1 cup almond flour
- 4 teaspoons almond oil
- 2 cups whole wheat flour
- ¼ cup vital wheat gluten

- 1 teaspoon xanthan gum
- 2 ¼ teaspoons package dry yeast

16 Slices/2 pounds
- ½ cup honey
- 1 ½ cups water
- 1 ½ teaspoon salt
- 1 ½ cup almond flour
- 4 ½ teaspoons almond oil
- 2 ½ cups whole wheat flour
- ½ cup vital wheat gluten
- 1 ½ teaspoon xanthan gum
- 2 ½ teaspoons package dry yeast

Directions:
1. Place ingredients in the bread machine pan according to the manufacturer's recommended order.
2. Select the appropriate setting with preferable loaf size on your bread machine, and press Start.
3. When the bread is done, unplug the machine and remove the pan.
4. Gently shake the bucket to remove the bread, and place it on a cooling rack.
5. Slice after 10 minutes and enjoy!

Nutrition:
Per Serving Calories: 117, Total Fat: 2g, Saturated Fat: 0g, Carbohydrates: 22g, Fiber: 3g, Sodium: 206mg, Protein: 5g

Tip: You can substitute almond oil with coconut or sunflower oil in case of availability issues.

147. Semisweet Chocolate Bread

Prep Time: 5 minutes or less
Ready Time: 2 hours 50 minutes

12 Slices/1 ½ pounds
- 1 egg
- 1 cup milk
- ¼ cup water
- 1 teaspoon salt

- 3 cups bread flour
- 2 tablespoons white sugar
- 3 tablespoons brown sugar
- 1 teaspoon ground cinnamon
- 1 ½ teaspoons active dry yeast
- 2 tablespoons margarine, softened
- ¾ cup semisweet chocolate chips

16 Slices/2 pounds

- 2 eggs
- 1 ½ cups milk
- ½ cup water
- 1 ½ teaspoons salt
- 4 cups bread flour
- 2 ½ tablespoons white sugar
- 3 ½ tablespoons brown sugar
- 1 ½ teaspoon ground cinnamon
- 2 teaspoons active dry yeast
- 2 ½ tablespoons margarine, softened
- 1 cup semisweet chocolate chips

Directions:

1. Place ingredients in the bread machine pan according to the manufacturer's recommended order.
2. Select the Mix Bread setting which lets fruits, nuts, and seeds get mixed into the dough, choose Medium crust with preferable loaf size on your bread machine, and press Start.
3. When the bread is done, unplug the machine and remove the pan.
4. Gently shake the bucket to remove the bread, and place it on a cooling rack.
5. Slice after 10 minutes and enjoy!

Nutrition:
Per Serving Calories: 172, Total Fat: 5g, Saturated Fat: 2g, Carbohydrates: 28g, Fiber: 2g, Sodium: 189mg, Protein: 4g

Tip: Add frozen chocolate chips to avoid them from melting during the dough cycle.

148. White Potato Bread

Prep Time: 5 minutes or less
Ready Time: 1 hour 55 minutes

12 Slices/1 ½ pounds

- 1 ⅛ cups water
- 3 cups bread flour
- 1 ½ teaspoons salt
- ½ cup dry potato flakes
- 1 ½ tablespoons margarine
- 2 teaspoons active dry yeast
- 1 ½ tablespoons white sugar
- 1 ½ tablespoons instant powdered milk

16 Slices/2 pounds

- 1 ½ cups water
- 4 cups bread flour
- 2 teaspoons salt
- 1 cup dry potato flakes
- 2 tablespoons margarine
- 2 ½ teaspoons active dry yeast
- 2 tablespoons white sugar
- 2 tablespoons instant powdered milk

Directions:

1. Place ingredients in the bread machine pan according to the manufacturer's recommended order.
2. Select the Basic/White setting with preferable loaf size on your bread machine, and press Start.
3. When the bread is done, unplug the machine and remove the pan.
4. Gently shake the bucket to remove the bread, and place it on a cooling rack.
5. Slice after 10 minutes and enjoy!

Nutrition:
Per Serving Calories: 29, Total Fat: 1g, Saturated Fat: 0g, Carbohydrates: 4g, Fiber: 0g, Sodium: 312mg, Protein: 1g

Tip: You can use potato broth as a substitute for water and for added flavor.

149. Fragrant Garlic Bread

Prep Time: 5 minutes or less
Ready Time: 3 hours 5 minutes

12 Slices/1 ½ pounds

- 1 ½ cups water
- 1 ½ teaspoons salt
- 3 cups bread flour
- ½ teaspoon dried basil
- 2 ½ tablespoons olive oil
- ½ teaspoon garlic powder
- ½ teaspoon minced garlic
- 2 ½ tablespoons white sugar
- ⅛ cup grated Parmesan cheese
- 2 teaspoons bread machine yeast
- 2 ½ tablespoons chopped fresh chives
- ½ teaspoon coarsely ground black pepper

16 Slices/2 pounds

- 1 ⅜ cups water
- 2 teaspoons salt
- 4 cups bread flour
- 1 teaspoon dried basil
- 3 tablespoons olive oil
- 1 teaspoon garlic powder
- 1 teaspoon minced garlic
- 3 tablespoons white sugar
- ¼ cup grated Parmesan cheese
- 2 ½ teaspoons bread machine yeast
- 3 tablespoons chopped fresh chives
- 1 teaspoon coarsely ground black pepper

Directions:
1. Place ingredients in the bread machine pan according to the manufacturer's recommended order.
2. Select the Basic/White setting with preferable crust and loaf size on your bread machine, and press Start.
3. When the bread is done, unplug the machine and remove the pan.
4. Gently shake the bucket to remove the bread, and place it on a cooling rack.
5. Slice after 10 minutes and enjoy!

Nutrition:

Per Serving Calories: 175, Total Fat: 4g, Saturated Fat: 1g, Carbohydrates: 30g, Fiber: 1g, Sodium: 332mg, Protein: 5g

Tip: You can increase the quantity of basil and parmesan if you like a stronger flavor.

150. Hawaiian Pineapple Bread

Prep Time: 10 minutes or less
Ready Time: 3 hours 10 minutes

12 Slices/1 ½ pounds

- 1 egg
- ¼ cup milk
- ½ teaspoon salt
- ⅓ cup white sugar
- 3 cups bread flour
- ½ cup mashed banana
- ¼ cup margarine, softened
- 1 teaspoon coconut extract
- ½ cup instant potato flakes
- 1 ½ teaspoons active dry yeast
- ½ cup crushed pineapple, with juice

16 Slices/2 pounds

- 1 egg
- ½ cup milk
- 1 teaspoon salt
- ½ cup white sugar
- 4 cups bread flour
- 1 cup mashed banana
- ½ cup margarine, softened
- 1 ½ teaspoon coconut extract
- 1 cup instant potato flakes
- 2 teaspoons active dry yeast
- 1 cup crushed pineapple, with juice

Directions:
1. Place ingredients in the bread machine pan according to the manufacturer's recommended order.
2. Select the Light setting with preferable crust and loaf size on your bread machine, and press Start.
3. When the bread is done, unplug the machine and remove the pan.

4. Gently shake the bucket to remove the bread, and place it on a cooling rack.
5. Slice after 10 minutes and enjoy!

Nutrition:
Per Serving Calories: 169, Total Fat: 4g, Saturated Fat: 1g, Carbohydrates: 29g, Fiber: 1g, Sodium: 122mg, Protein: 4g

Tip: You can increase the quantity of milk if the dough is stiff and flour if the dough is too wet. It all depends on how soft you want the dough to get during the kneading cycle. The softer the dough, the nicer your bread will be.

151. Special Multigrain Bread

Prep Time: 10 minutes or less
Ready Time: 2 hours 55 minutes

12 Slices/1 ½ pounds
- 1 cup water
- 1 ½ teaspoons salt
- 1 ½ cups bread flour
- 1 ½ tablespoons millet
- 1 ½ tablespoons quinoa
- 1 ½ cups whole wheat flour
- 1 ½ tablespoons flax seeds
- ½ cup packed brown sugar
- 1 ½ tablespoons sesame seeds
- 1 ½ tablespoons dry milk powder
- 2 ½ tablespoons sunflower seeds
- 1 ½ tablespoons butter, softened
- 2 tablespoons bread machine yeast

16 Slices/2 pounds
- 1 ½ cup water
- 2 teaspoons salt
- 2 cups bread flour
- 2 tablespoons millet
- 2 tablespoons quinoa
- 2 cups whole wheat flour
- 2 tablespoons flax seeds
- ¾ cup packed brown sugar
- 2 tablespoons sesame seeds
- 2 tablespoons dry milk powder
- 3 tablespoons sunflower seeds
- 2 tablespoons butter, softened

- 2 ½ tablespoons bread machine yeast

Directions:
1. Place ingredients In the bread machine pan according to the manufacturer's recommended order.
2. Select the appropriate setting with preferable crust and loaf size on your bread machine, and press Start.
3. When the bread is done, unplug the machine and remove the pan.
4. Gently shake the bucket to remove the bread, and place it on a cooling rack.
5. Slice after 10 minutes and enjoy!

Nutrition:
Per Serving Calories: 124, Total Fat: 2g, Saturated Fat: 1g, Carbohydrates: 23g, Fiber: 1g, Sodium: 207mg, Protein: 4g

Tip: To turn this bread into 100% whole grain, you can use spelt flour instead of bread flour for personal preference.

152. Simple Sugar Free Bread

Prep Time: 10 minutes or less
Ready Time: 2 hours 55 minutes

12 Slices/1 ½ pounds
- ½ teaspoon salt
- ½ teaspoon cinnamon
- 1 tablespoon olive oil
- 2 cups all-purpose flour
- 2 tablespoons warm water
- 1 cup skim milk, lukewarm
- 1 ¼ cups whole wheat flour
- 2 ¼ teaspoons active dry yeast

16 Slices/2 pounds
- 1 teaspoon salt
- 1 teaspoon cinnamon
- 1 ½ tablespoon olive oil
- 3 cups all-purpose flour
- 2 ½ tablespoons warm water
- 1 ½ cups skim milk, lukewarm
- 1 ½ cups whole wheat flour
- 2 ½ teaspoons active dry yeast

Directions:

1. Place ingredients In the bread machine pan according to the manufacturer's recommended order.
2. Select the Light setting with preferable crust and loaf size on your bread machine, and press Start.
3. When the bread is done, unplug the machine and remove the pan.
4. Gently shake the bucket to remove the bread, and place it on a cooling rack.
5. Slice after 10 minutes and enjoy!

Nutrition:

Per Serving Calories: 110, Total Fat: 1g, Saturated Fat: 0g, Carbohydrates: 21g, Fiber: 2g, Sodium: 86mg, Protein: 4g

Tip: This is a versatile low salt bread, use it for spreads or have with baked beans for dinner.

Conclusion

As you have seen, a bread machine can be a versatile and convenient tool for making delicious homemade bread. Whether you are an expert baker or just starting out, a bread machine can help you achieve great results with minimal effort. From classic white bread to specialty loaves and even desserts, the possibilities are endless. As you explore the recipes in this cookbook, don't be afraid to be creative to experiment and make adjustments to suit your taste and preferences. With a little practice and creativity, you can customize your bread to create unique and delicious creations that you will be proud to share with family and friends.

Remember, making bread is not only about the end result but also about the process of creating something with your own hands. There's something truly satisfying about the aroma of fresh bread baking in your home and the joy of slicing into a warm loaf that you have made yourself. So, let this cookbook be your guide as you embark on a journey of bread-making with your trusty bread machine. Enjoy the process, experiment, and, most importantly, have fun!

But wait, Hold on!

There are more surprises coming your way:

BONUS 1: Digital version of this book which includes also the 8 slices/ 1 pound version of all recipes

BONUS 2: Dips & Recipes 40 mouthwatering recipes for every occasion

BONUS 3: Recipe Card: Your Recipe Journey Starts Here - Blank Canvas, Endless Possibilities

The bonuses are 100% FREE

You only need to provide your name and email; no additional information is required.

Unlock your exclusive bonuses NOW by scanning the QR code!

Or go to www.bookisho.com/bread-amazon

Bonus Chapter

Cleaning And Maintenance of a Bread Machine

Regularly cleaning your bread machine is essential to maintain its longevity and ensure that your bread is free from any residue or dirt. To clean your bread machine effectively, start by unplugging it and making sure it is cool to the touch. Next, remove the bread pan and kneading paddle from the machine. Check the manufacturer's instructions to see if they are dishwasher-safe. If not, wash them by hand using warm soapy water and a soft sponge or small soft brush. Avoid using any abrasive material that could scratch the non-stick surface of the pan. Dry the pan and paddle thoroughly before reassembling.

After cleaning the bread pan and kneading the paddle, use a lightly damp cloth to wipe down the interior and exterior of the machine. Be careful to avoid getting water into the heating element or any other electrical components. Use a soft damp cloth or some sponge to clean the lid and viewing window, and if there is any baked-on residue, use a non-abrasive cleaner to remove it. Remember to also clean the control panel by wiping it down with a slightly damp cloth. Avoid getting water into any of the buttons or display screens. Once every part of your bread machine is clean and dry, reassemble the bread machine and plug it back in.

It's important to note that you should never submerge the bread machine in water or use harsh chemicals to clean it. Doing so can cause great damage to the machine. If you are unsure about how to clean your specific model of the bread machine, consult the instruction manual or contact the manufacturer for guidance. Regular cleaning of your bread machine is an easy and effective way to keep it working optimally and producing delicious, clean bread for years to come.

How Do You Store Your Bread Machine?

Proper storage of a bread machine is important if you are not planning to use it for a long time or if you need to store it temporarily. To protect it from damage, there are several steps you can take. First, make sure the machine is clean and dry before storing it. Follow the cleaning instructions provided in the manual or by the manufacturer. It's important to remove any bread crumbs or debris that may be stuck in the machine, especially around the kneading paddle. Use a small brush or a soft cloth to do this.

If possible, disassemble the machine by removing the bread pan and kneading the paddle, and storing them separately. This will help to prevent any damage that may occur during transportation or storage. When choosing a suitable storage location, consider a dry, cool, and clean area that's not exposed to direct sunlight, high humidity, or extreme temperatures. Additionally, ensure that the machine is not exposed to any potential hazards, such as water or dust.

To further protect the bread machine, cover it with a clean cloth or plastic bag. This will help to prevent it from accumulating dust and other potential hazards. Finally, place the bread machine in its storage location and make sure it's stable and won't be knocked over or damaged. If necessary, secure it with tape or straps to prevent movement during transportation.

Country White Bread 14

Milk & Honey Bread 14

Simple Bread Recipe 14

Cinnamon Bread..15

Milky White Buttery Bread 16

Molasses Rye Bread 16

Sweet Basic Bread 17

Cornmeal Bread 17

Peanut Butter Bread 18

Onion Bread 18

Everyday Half Wheat Bread 19

Spelt Everyday Bread 19

Oatmeal Everyday Bread..20

Cocoa Whole Wheat Bread 21

Cajun Classic Bread 21

Quinoa & Whole Wheat Bread 22

Whole Wheat Bread with Flaxseed..........................22

Herbed Whole Wheat Bread Recipe 23

Sweet Potato Bread 23

Black & Green Olive Whole Wheat Bread 24

Sesame Whole Wheat Bread 25

Whole Wheat Cinnamon Raisin Bread 25

Whole Wheat Bread with Sunflower Seed 26

Simple Whole Wheat Bread 26

Whole Grain Seed Loaf 27

Whole Wheat Banana Bread......................................27

French Bread with A Crust 28

Bran Bread with Oat...28

Tomato & Olive Bread 29

Amish White Bread Loaf 29

Lightweight Oat Bread 30

Whole Grain Wheat Bread 30

Soft Everyday Bread 31

Caraway Rye Bread Loaf..31

Simple Breakfast Milk Bread 32

Potato Crust Bread Loaf 32

Breakfast Cranberry & Orange Bread 33

Flaxseed Whole Wheat Bread...................................33

Sunflower Seed Bran Bread 34

Garlic Herb Bread..35

Italian Herb & Cheese Bread 35

Potato Whole Wheat Bread 36

Kalamata Olive Oil Bread 36

Star Anise Seed Bread 37

Orange Spice Bread...37

Toasted Walnut Bread 38

Chives & Sour Cream Bread 39

Caramelized Onion & Yeast Bread 39

Sunflower Seed Yeast Bread 40

Cajun Herb Bread 40

Roasted Garlic Clove Bread..41

Rosemary Italian Peasant Bread 42

Cream Cheese Yeast Bread 43

Sharp Cheese Yeast Bread 43

Feta Cheese Yeast Bread 44

Jalapeno & Cheese Bread 44

Ricotta Cheese & Yeast Bread 45

Pepperoni & Cheese Bread 45

Cottage Cheese & Dill Bread 46

Simple Oregano & Cheese Bread...................................46

Cheese & Scallion Bread 47

Easy Cottage Cheese Bread 47

Cheese Bread with Pepperoni 48

Cheese Bread with Jalapeno 48

Bacon & Cheddar Cheese Bread 49

Pumpkin Spice Quick Bread 50

Cranberry Quick Bread Loaf..50

Zucchini Quick Bread Loaf...51

Quick Banana Bread Loaf..51

Classic White Bread with No Yeast 52

Cornmeal Quick Bread 52

No Yeast Quick Flatbread 53

No Yeast Tutti Frutti Bread Cake 53

Pumpkin Pie Spice Quick Bread 54

Jalapeno Cheese Quick Cornbread 55

Yeast Free Quick Chocolate Cake 55

Moist Quick Chocolate Cake 56

Quick Zucchini Bread Loaf...56

Nutty Banana Bread..58

Date Bread with Cinnamon...58

Pumpernickel Bread 59

Cream Cheese Sweet Bread..59

Sweet Fruit Bread 60

Cranberry & Oats Bread..61

Applesauce & Oat Bread 61

Sweet Orange & Cranberry Bread 62

Sweet Portuguese Bread 62

Sweet Rum Raisin Bread 63

Sweet & Spicy Fruit Bread 63

Pecan & Raisin Bread 64

Cherry & Pecan Bread 65

Easy Gluten Free Bread...66

Healthy Gluten Free Bread 66

Einkorn Spelt Flour Bread 67

Whole Grain Gluten Free Bread 67

Raisin Bran Bread Loaf 68

Almond High Protein Bread 98

Amish Sourdough Bread 88

Basic Sourdough Bread 85

Bread Machine Sourdough 83

Caramelized Onion Focaccia Bread 79

Carrot & Thyme Yeast Bread 90

Cereal Grain Bread 92

Cheesy Rosemary Bread 96

Chocolate & Cinnamon Bread 92

Christmas Limpa Bread 94

Cornbread Gluten Free Loaf 72

Czech Sourdough Bread 87

Easy Molasses Loaf Bread 95

Easy Sourdough Bread 83

Focaccia Flat Bread 81

Fragrant Garlic Bread 99

Gluten Free Almond Bread 69

Gluten Free White Bread 68

Golden Syrup Bread 93

Hawaiian Pineapple Bread 100

Healthy Einkorn Bread Loaf 97

Herb Focaccia Bread 77

Italian Pizza Crust 76

Linseed Gluten Free Bread 71

Moist Peanut Butter Bread 91

Multigrain Sourdough Bread 86

Oat Rice Gluten Free Bread 70

Oatmeal & Honey Multigrain Bread 91

Olive Focaccia Bread 80

Onion & Cheese Focaccia 79

Onion & Herbs Focaccia 81

Overnight Sourdough Bread 87

Persimmon Pulp Bread 96

Pure Whole Wheat Bread 90

Quick Banana Nut Bread 97

Rice Gluten Free Bread 73

Rosemary & Garlic Focaccia 77

Rosemary Sourdough Bread 84

Rye Sourdough Bread 84

Semisweet Chocolate Bread 98

Simple Gluten Free Bread 70

Simple Pizza Bread Machine Dough 74

Simple Sugar Free Bread 101

Sourdough Bread with A Twist 86

Sourdough Bread with Beer 88

Sourdough Bread with Oatmeal 89

Sourdough Pizza Dough Bread 75

Sparkling Water Pizza Dough 75

Special Multigrain Bread 101

Special Panettone Bread 94

Sun-Dried Tomato Focaccia Bread 78

Super Easy Pizza Bread 74

Tangy Sourdough Bread 83

Vegan Bread Machine Loaf 71

White Potato Bread 99

Zucchini Whole Wheat Bread 93

Printed in Great Britain
by Amazon

44880338R00059